THE QUEEN MOTHER

Alastair Burnet

MICHAEL O'MARA BOOKS LIMITED
in association with
INDEPENDENT TELEVISION NEWS LIMITED

First published in Great Britain by Independent Television News Ltd in association with Michael O'Mara Books Ltd, 1985

Revised and extended edition published 1990

ISBN 1–85479–016–1

Designed by Martin Bristow

Video film processed by BPCC Video Graphics
Typeset by Bookworm Typesetting, Manchester
Printed and bound in Spain by Graficas Estella, S.A. Navarra

Front endpaper: Continuing the custom begun by Queen Alexandra, the Queen Mother distributed shamrock to the Irish Guards on St Patrick's Day, 1984

Rear endpaper: The Queen Mother at Sandringham Flower Show

Half title: The Queen Mother on her 87th birthday at Clarence House, photographed by Lord Snowdon

Frontispiece: The Queen Mother surrounded by her grandchildren, Prince Charles, Prince Edward, Princess Anne and Prince Andrew, specially photographed for her 85th birthday by Norman Parkinson

Acknowledgments

Unless otherwise acknowledged, the photographs in this book are the copyright of Independent Television News. Additional photographs are reproduced by kind pemission of the following:

Alpha: 116, 117; Camera Press: half title, 8, 9, 51, 85 (top), 90, 94, 95, 97, 98, 103; (Cecil Beaton): front jacket (bottom right), 41, 42, 64 (below), 65; (Anthony Buckley): 61, (ILN): 12, 20; (Norman Parkinson): 2, 18-19, 66, 67, 68, 69 (above and below); (James Reid): 54-55; (Snowdon): 6-7; Gerry Craham: 79; Lionel Cherruault: 107 (top left); John Curtis/ITN: 88; Tim Graham: endpapers, 11, 27, 73 (above and below), 74, 81, 82, 84 (top), 89, 102, 107 (bottom left and right), 108, 110, 111, 112, 113, 118, 119, 120; Robert Harding Picture Library: 32; Reproduced by Gracious Permission of Her Majesty the Queen: back jacket (top left); Hulton-Deutsch: front jacket (top right and bottom left); Anwar Hussein: 71 (below), 72, 83, 86, 105 (bottom right), 115; Illustrated London News: front jacket (top middle): 13, 15, 22 (left), 36, 37, 38, 39; Photographers International: front jacket (bottom middle), back jacket, 105 (top right), 107 (top right), 109; Popperfoto: 91, 92, 93, 96, 99, 100, 101, 104 (left and right), 106 (top), 114; Syndication International: 16, 17, 22 (right), 23, 24, 25 (above and below), 30, 33, 34, 35, 44, 45, 46, 48, 49, 56, 57, 58-59, 64 (above), 70, 71 (top), 105 (top and bottom left), 106 (bottom); Topham: 31, 47, 60.

Contents

CHAPTER ONE
Her Life's Work 6

CHAPTER TWO
The Queen from Scotland 20

CHAPTER THREE
'The intolerable honour' 30

CHAPTER FOUR
'I shall not go down' 44

CHAPTER FIVE
The Austerity Monarchy 52

CHAPTER SIX
'Isn't it exciting!' 60

Birthdays Past 64

CHAPTER SEVEN
'How are my darlings?' 74

CHAPTER EIGHT
'That valiant woman' 80

CHAPTER NINE
Her Contribution to History 88

Royal Style 104

CHAPTER TEN
The Unending Test 108

CHAPTER ONE

Her Life's Work

She is as old as the century. She has weathered its wars and its ways better than the century has. What was taken for granted in the world on August 4, 1900 has been turned upside down, but in those eighty-five years nothing has been more extraordinary than the success of her life's work.

Most of the population of Britain lives in the permanent illusion that they have met her personally. They talk about her as if they had; they enjoy her successes; they feel for her in disappointments; and they smile knowingly about her few foibles. They like to see her in the winner's enclosure at Sandown races, collecting a cup for a change. They enjoy the idea of her insisting on more spirits being stirred into a naval pudding, or clambering in and out of gondolas on the canals of Venice at her age, or receiving the children's posies at the gates of Clarence House on her birthday, or smiling, with the patience of much practice, through a lengthy after-dinner speech by the Life President of Malawi at Windsor Castle. They think they know what she's thinking. And, quite possibly, they are right.

They admire her for her tireless attendance on themselves, for all the buildings she has opened, the ribbons cut, the cords pulled, the command performances bravely endured, the launching and the lunching. They admire even more the punctiliousness about what matters to plain people: her visit to black Railton Road in Brixton, her care for the Irish Guards every St Patrick's Day, her courage on her husband's death, her ceaseless work for the bombed-out in the Blitz. They are possessive of her, of whether she has chosen blue or pink for her visit today, of her wave, of her smile that never falters, of her hats, of her handshake, of the good weather she is known always to arrange, of the sparkle she gives unsparingly to others. She is not known for her speeches, but there has built up around her a popular collection of her thoughts and sayings, especially in the war, which have always brought comfort and encouragement. She happens to enjoy talking to people; she shows it and they know it. She enjoys her public engagements and seldom, if ever, leaves early. She knows people's language, and she has their number. They don't mind that she does. They have known her quite a time now. She is herself, unique. There has been no other.

All in all, it may even be true that nearly everyone in Britain has met her, or, for that matter, nearly everyone in Europe, the Commonwealth and the United States put together has met her. She would have been a personality in any age. But it is this age that produced her, an age of discontent and war, intent perhaps more than any other on sweeping away the past and its symbols and memories. It is in such an age that she has become, without hyperbole, a symbol of the century and an adornment to her part of it.

When she was fourteen, at eleven pm on her birthday, Great Britain went to war with Germany – the Great War that was to bring down the monarchies of the Hapsburgs, the Hohenzollerns and the Romanovs.

When she was eighteen, a girl at her coming-out dance in the society that had survived the war, little seemed less likely than that monarchy,

Queen Elizabeth with her daughters the Princesses Elizabeth and Margaret at Windsor in 1941.

effective monarchy, would persist in Britain – far less strengthen its place in plain people's minds – through the century.

When she was thirty-six, brought by Edward VIII's abdication to the throne neither she nor her husband had wished for, nothing seemed less likely than that their reign would be so consistently popular – or essential to the success of the British people in their last war as a world power.

When she was fifty-three and her daughter was crowned, little seemed less likely than that, in a country having to bring itself to accept that it was coming down in the world, the reputation of the monarch would grow as steadily as Empire, influence, and industrial output would, relatively, diminish.

The twentieth century has settled for her, and her husband's, idea of monarchy. Her daughter has carried it out in her own way, the daughter of a shy, good and modest man, accomplishing in her long reign what he began in his brief one. But the style was set by the Queen's parents, and by what they led the country to expect of them. This was not what the intellectuals and socialites had expected or wished for. The modern monarchy grew from George VI's understanding of his duty and his own uncertainty. It grew, too, from his wife's understanding of his decency and his strengths. Because she got that right, she made him, and the monarchy, the central, cohesive spine of the country once more – a country which faced, in turn, a

Previous page: The Christening of Prince Henry, October, 1984.

The King and Queen with their daughters acknowledge the cheer of the crowd celebrating the victory over Japan on August 15, 1945.

desperate war, near bankruptcy, industrial inadequacy, and a conviction that it owed itself a more comfortable life.

When the British know what they want they are both demanding of their politicians and unforgiving of their failures. Of their royal family, over the years, they ask for little. They do not demand that the Princess of Wales makes brilliant public speeches. They simply believe in her and dote on her every appearance. They are ready to forgive almost anything. Princess Anne, the scapegoat, has been long forgotten. She is now admired entirely on her own merits. None of this could have happened had not someone patiently, shrewdly and tirelessly made the royal family into a success. The British have no doubt about who that someone is.

Lady Elizabeth Bowes-Lyon was the first commoner to marry close to the throne since the first, ill-judged marriage of the Duke of York who was to become James II and VII. She was the first wholly British queen for centuries, and the first Scottish queen the English have ever had.

These originalities have mattered more than anyone could have suspected on her wedding day in 1923. In marrying as he did, the Duke of York took the monarchy out of the minor kingdoms and principalities – Saxe-Coburg-Gotha, Denmark, Teck – that had been suitable and even popular for the nineteenth-century empire. He did not dream of putting loyalty and affection to the test in the way his

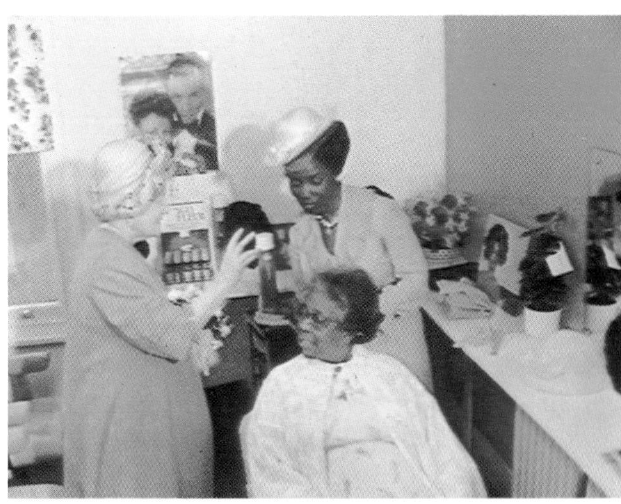

Above: Calypso music played as the Queen Mother arrived in Brixton for her now famous visit. Although her security men wanted her to move quickly indoors, she wanted to meet the people – and she did. Once inside the Brixton Centre she chatted with many of the local ladies about domestic pursuits.

elder brother did when he chose, with the smart set's approval, a twice-divorced American from Baltimore.

She was the youngest daughter of a large, gregarious, wealthy and happy family. The charm, the warmth, the sympathy that the Strathmores' lives personified were brought by her, the favourite of the family, to the stiff, dull, rather humdrum court of George V and Queen Mary, whose inability to communicate their own affection for their four sons was to exact a high price from all of them. George V, for once acknowledging a merit in his second son, simply adored her.

The Queen Mother, accompanied by the Princess of Wales and the Duchess of York, greeting locals at Sandringham on Christmas Day, 1988.

He believed Bertie would be lucky to get her, fretted over the courtship and after the marriage even – greatest of favours – put up with her unpunctuality. And she, it was to become clear, was learning from him.

She was a child of the country, of that democratic countryside of Strathmore, centred on Glamis and all its memories, that first taught her how to get on with all manner of people; and four years nursing the wounded of the Great War instilled in her a sympathy not always evident in royal persons. *The Times,* patronisingly, said on her wedding that people knew 'very little about her, as of necessity they know very little about well-bred young ladies living quietly at home'. Her friends knew of her vitality and sincerity, but to London eyes she dressed unfashionably, as she was, charmingly, to do all her life. All of which made her perfect for Bertie: life's greatest favour to him was that it was a love match.

What was also to matter was that she entered the royal family when the demand for a popular, family monarchy was gathering pace – and there was not all that much of a popular family to put on show. There was certainly the Prince of Wales, her brother-in-law, the favourite of the nation. But he was not married, and showed no sign of getting married. His two younger brothers were not to be married until 1934 and 1935. The Victorian constitutionalist, Walter Bagehot, as all royal advisers knew, had said a family on the throne was 'an interesting idea'. But royal weddings were scarce, so George V shrewdly

Opposite: Lady Elizabeth Bowes-Lyon. A picture which appeared in the Wedding edition of the Illustrated London News, April 28, 1923.

encouraged them. He was aware that 'the women – one half the human race at least – care fifty times more for a marriage than a ministry'.

Lady Elizabeth Bowes-Lyon became only the third royal bride to be married at Westminster Abbey since 1382. She had been a bridesmaid at the Princess Royal's wedding there the year before, in 1922. She thereby entered public life precisely when the cinema and the popular pictorial press were coming into their own, increasingly dependent on a royal family, and its ceremonies, to build audiences and circulations. It was not thought proper to have her wedding broadcast on the wireless – George V had not even begun his regular Christmas broadcasts – but film of the wedding procession was shown in Britain south of the Tyne that night. It was only a foretaste of a life that would be lived never far from a camera. This publicity was not what she wanted, but it was what the imperatives of a monarchy surviving into a democratic age required. The quiet life that the Duke and Duchess of York preferred for themselves and their children was not going to be. And when she had her two children, Elizabeth in 1926 and Margaret Rose in 1930, there were no other royal children close to the throne.

The public attention on all royal occasions was on them and their family. And they were a delightful family; the country doted on them. It made up for the rumours that were beginning, slowly, to spread about the Prince of Wales. In the end, it was not just George V who wished that his eldest son would never marry 'and that nothing will come between Bertie and Lilibet and the throne'. But, again, that was not what the Duchess of York wanted if it meant an impossible strain on her husband, as it was to.

Below: Lady Elizabeth Bowes-Lyon leaving 17 Bruton Street, her London home, for her wedding to the Duke of York in Westminster Abbey on April 26, 1923.

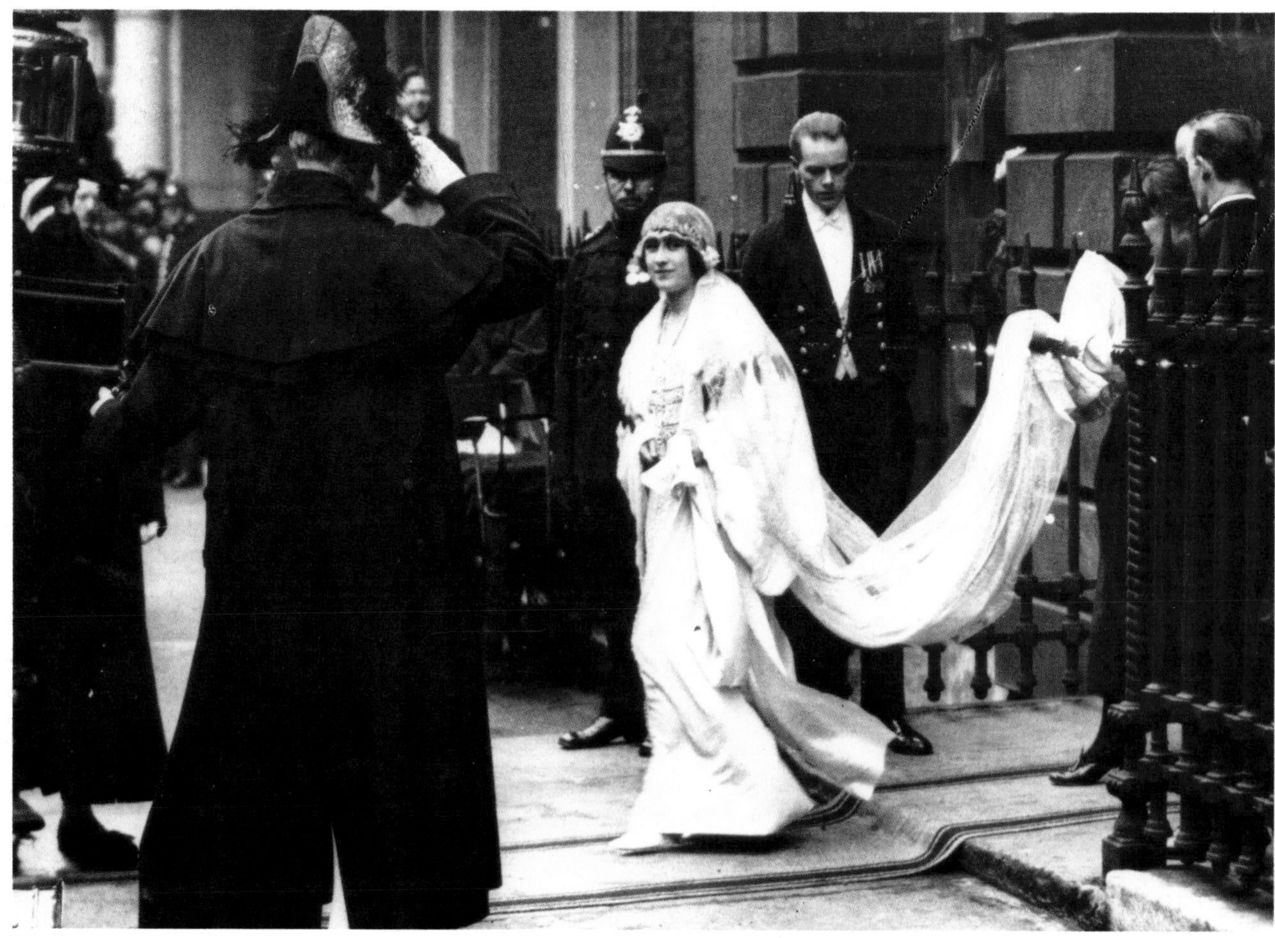

The Duchess knew from the beginning that even the modest royal duties that they were asked to do at home and in the Empire would be a constant worry because of her husband's bad stammer. Opening the Empire Exhibition at Wembley in 1925 was agonising for them both, and all the more because the long pauses in his speech happened under his father's disappointed gaze. It was she who persuaded the Duke to see the Australian specialist, Lionel Logue, made him persevere, practised with him, and gave him confidence. The stammer did not go, but he could now cope with it; it even became endearing to a country willing him to go on in the darkest days of the war. Her success in that may even have been her greatest single contribution, among so many contributions, to the future of the crown.

For in the radio age the voice of the sovereign suddenly mattered, as it had never mattered with Victoria or Edward VII. George V started it: his voice, grandfatherly, reassuring, patently sincere, came over well. It was not exactly what he said as the way that he said it. His four short Christmas talks were so popular that it was the photograph of the King at the microphone, talking to his people, and not of the King with the crown on his head, that became his own and the accepted image of the democratic monarchy.

So when, at Edward VIII's Abdication, the capability of the Duke of York to succeed his brother was briefly questioned, it was not on the ground of his inexperience of public life – his interest in labour relations, so appropriate in the Britain of the general strike and the great slump, had led to him being called 'the shop steward' by the rest of the family – but on the continuing doubt that an ineffective speaker, especially on the radio, might prejudice the monarchy's recovery from the loss of a once so popular king. It was only a passing doubt, but it had been the Duchess's patient persistence years before that helped to make it so. George VI spoke directly to his people by radio on the evening after his coronation, the first time a monarch had done so. His confidence grew, audibly. He was, indeed, to produce the most memorable passage of all royal radio talks: 'I said to the man who stood at the gate of the year . . .'. His success was hers.

As war approached in 1939 it was the royal family, the pictorial royal family whose virtues were her virtues, that was seen to matter all the more to the confidence and self-respect of the country. In the cinema newsreels it was the King and Queen and their daughters, with their dogs and ponies in the English countryside or arriving for their summer holidays at Balmoral, that became all the more important in national policy as a contrast to the orating, unmarried and childless Nazi dictator, Hitler.

Britain saw itself fighting for the family and its blessings; and the world, especially the United States, saw Britain in that light too. Nothing had helped more in encouraging that American view than the almost homely meeting of the King and Queen with the Roosevelts, picnicking on the President's front porch at Hyde Park, New York, in June, 1939, with war only months away, the first visit of a reigning British monarch to the United States.

Because she was who she was, these things were not contrived. Her first thought for her daughters was that they should have a happy home, as she had done: a Christian one, based on sufficient discipline and much love and trust. She chose not to push them into the higher reaches of education, as she had not been pushed. She wanted them

Opposite: The Duke and Duchess of York on their wedding day, April 26, 1923.

Opposite: Part of the Royal pair's honeymoon was spent at Polesden Lacey in Surrey

'to spend as long as possible in the open air, to enjoy to the full the pleasures of the country, to be able to dance and draw and appreciate music, to acquire good manners and perfect deportment, and to cultivate all the distinctively feminine graces.' That would soon come to seem old-fashioned, as, to some, it did then; it happened to be integral to her idea of the world they would grow up in and of the duties life would impose on them. It was cautious, sensible, percipient. It also worked. It produced a Queen who has reigned, to the increasing pleasure and pride of the country, for over 30 successful years, and a royal family that is a real family. Through the daily life of the crown, Britain has identified itself with a simple and satisfying family life: an image and a reputation that would have greatly surprised almost all earlier royal generations.

It is a British fallacy to believe that all this just came about naturally, a family acquired by the nation as it once supposed it acquired an empire: in a fit of absence of mind. Nothing was less true. It was not easy. It had to be worked for over the years. The British enjoy their family all the more when, as in all families, things go a little awry. When the light that beats upon the throne turns out to be camera lights; when television and the newspapers are on the look-out for every rumour and minor drama, for a wrong word or an imagined slight; when the world is watching for signs of pique or boredom,

Right: The Duke and Duchess of York waving to the crowd from the balcony of their home in Piccadilly on their return from the Empire Tour, June 28, 1927.
Overleaf: Norman Parkinson's study of the Queen Mother and her daughters on her 80th birthday.

nothing is easy. They have all watched in vain for such signs in the Queen Mother.

Character has done it, and will-power. From the day of her wedding onwards, she has not been seen to falter, except for her brief withdrawal, when she acquired her retreat on the far coast of Caithness, the Castle of Mey, after George VI's death. When she returned it was as if she had never gone away. It may have been, for no one can tell, that the reluctant Queen, called on to work to save the monarchy after her brother-in-law's behaviour had come close to destroying it, and seeing her husband's years cut short because of it, had resolved that nothing she would do would prejudice what they had built up together.

In her daughter she had the fullest trust. Yet in the early years of Queen Elizabeth II the touch was by no means as assured as it was to become, or as, in retrospect, it has come to seem. Once the false adulation of the new Elizabethan age had died away, the intelligentsia moved in to criticise. The Queen Mother was not needed to rescue anyone or anything again. But she must always have known that she did mean continuity, respect and popularity, assets not lightly to be given up in any job. So she found, as if by instinct, her place in her daughter's retinue. The British constitution has no place for Queen Mothers, except, occasionally, as aspiring regents. Its society has certainly had no place for active Queen Mothers; the very deaf Queen Alexandra and the rather aloof Queen Mary had respect, as old age brings, or used to bring, respect among the British, but their public life was limited, their appearances grew ever fewer. Now there was a young Queen Mother of only fifty-two, energetic, well-informed, whom plain people would not allow to go away into retirement.

Never before had there even been a Queen Mother with a reigning Queen on the throne. It might have been difficult. That it never occurred to the world, or to them, that it would be difficult with this Queen and this Queen Mother was the further, decisive justification of the family and its upbringing. She had told her daughters: 'Your work is the rent you pay for life', a thought that would not have occurred to her husband's grandfather. It was what she had taught herself, and she was true to it.

In this making, or remaking, of the monarchy, she has often had to make her own way – not a lonely way, for her family has always been with her and close to her – but bringing her own common sense and flair to a job that can never be completed. The monarchy has been fortunate that its first commoner in centuries turned out to have the devotion and intelligence it needed. She has had her own resources of mind and strength. From her father-in-law, a wholly democratic king who never quite admitted it to himself, she learned that democracy insisted on adaptability, that old ceremonies and new techniques of communication could give more to the monarchy than they would take away, but that democracy requires duty and integrity – qualities in which his eldest son was found lacking. From her husband she learned that decency and devotion were qualities for a modern age, that courage could be shown in years of duty and sacrifice as surely as in battle. From her daughter, the Queen, she learned that her own life's work had been well done. From the country she has worked so long for too, she has learned that the one reward that matters, the reward that is freely given to her, is love.

CHAPTER TWO

The Queen from Scotland

She was born in England; her mother was an Englishwoman. Her chief nurseries were English. One was at St Paul's Walden Bury, in Hertfordshire, where she and her younger brother, David, lived in the enchanted woods in which, in their children's world, all fairy stories were true. The other was in her father's town house, 20 St James's Square, where she slept, on the night of her fourteenth birthday, excited both by the variety show at the London Coliseum she had just seen and by the rowdy demonstrations of the crowds there welcoming the inevitable declaration of war against Germany.

She first met her future husband at a party at Montague House, in Portman Square, in 1905 at which she, aged five, gave him, aged nine,

Right: Lady Elizabeth Bowes-Lyon, daughter of the 14th Earl of Strathmore, was born on August 4, 1900.

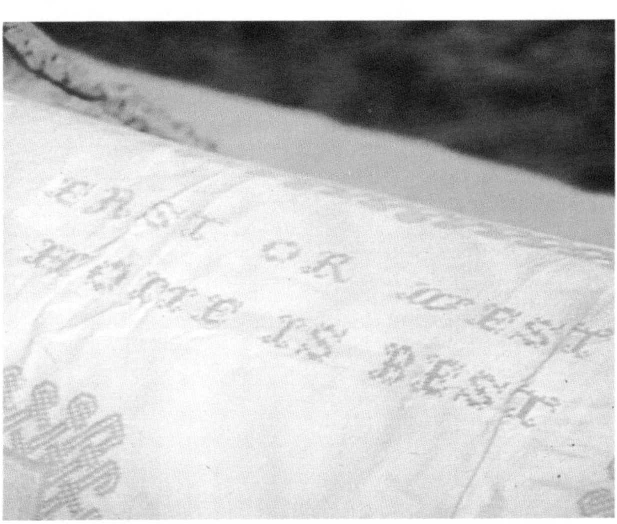

Above left: Glamis, the fairy-tale Scottish castle in the hills of Tayside and the childhood home of Lady Elizabeth Bowes-Lyon.
Below left: The sitting room at Glamis Castle has remained unchanged since the early days of the Queen Mother's marriage.
Above right: A portrait of the young Lady Elizabeth superimposed on the gardens of Glamis Castle.
Below right: A homely detail from the Queen Mother's sitting room.

the crystallised cherries from her piece of sugar cake. When they next met it was at a dance at 6 Grosvenor Square, in May, 1920. She accepted his second proposal of marriage at Walden Bury on Sunday, January 14, 1923, when, everyone else being at church, they took a walk through the woods of her childhood. She was married from her parents' new rented London home at 17 Bruton Street, Mayfair (now demolished), on April 26, 1923; and it was there that she gave birth to her first daughter on April 21, 1926. The first enjoyable family home that her husband and she had was at 145 Piccadilly (also now demolished). Accession to the throne in 1936 merely meant the family moved south across the Green Park to Buckingham Palace, so close that the young Princess Margaret Rose, who preferred the old home, proposed that a secret tunnel could be contrived between the two. Widowhood took her 200 yards down the Mall to Clarence House.

If anyone could be claimed by London and the home counties as of right, it would be her. She speaks highly, and enjoyably, of both. Yet there has never been any doubt at any stage of her life that she has been, is, and intends to remain, unchallengeably Scottish. This has been a matter of allegiance to her father and her ancestors; a matter of character and of instinctive sympathy for the people and the countryside with whom she has always felt most at home. In those windy spaces she has always known that she has been with her own, with the blood of her blood and bone of her bone. It gave her,

Left: A charming portrait of Lady Elizabeth aged 6.
Right: Lady Elizabeth Bowes-Lyon, then aged 9, with her brother David in fancy dress at Glamis Castle.

officially a commoner, a background and a pride that meant she need never be overawed by her in-laws' history. She has always had her history on her side. After all, she is descended from a king, Robert II of Scotland, whose predecessor, Robert the Bruce, saw the English off.

Her father's Scottish home, Glamis Castle, standing in the middle of green Strathmore, in what used to be called Forfarshire, was at the crossroads of everyone and everything going up the east coast of Scotland from the time of the Picts to the building of the Highland railway line in the nineteenth century. Indeed Glamis Castle has had as much history as any family, however royal, could want. This the young Elizabeth Bowes-Lyon drew into her very being every August when the family – the clan, they called themselves – travelled north to entertain, and shoot, and play cricket in the season.

Edwardian and Victorian recollections of existence in the great houses in August are replete with the boredom of the women. That was not true of the Lady Elizabeth. To her Glamis was, naturally, a castle of ghosts and monsters and, even more, of a history that she sensed and understood. There were the Mad Earl, the mysterious Beardie, the White Lady and the mild-mannered Grey Lady; all the stuff of impressionable house parties. But it went far beyond that. Malcolm II was murdered there; and Shakespeare (who might have stopped there) insisted that Duncan was too. Mary, Queen of Scots, stayed on her way to put down Huntly's rising in 1562. The Old Pretender, James VIII that never was, certainly stayed in 1716 after Sherriffmuir and even touched for the scrofula, the king's evil, in the chapel – apparently with success. Bonnie Prince Charlie may have been there in the Forty-Five; without question Cumberland was, on his way to Culloden. Cumberland's host smashed his bed when he left.

All this left its mark on Lady Elizabeth. Friends remember how she dressed up as the Princess Elizabeth, daughter of James VI and I, briefly the Winter Queen of Bohemia. She enjoyed the part: the evocation of the past was part of her. On these impressions and memories came the Great War. She was taken north that August to a house that was to become a hospital for the wounded and the convalescent. She was to help to care for them, nurse them. She has remembered it as a time when, amid intermittent lessons, she was 'so busy knitting, knitting, knitting'. There her mother and she heard the news of the death of one of her brothers in 1915 and of another badly wounded and taken prisoner in 1917. There, one testing day, she organised the house to fight a fire, calling out three brigades: the local one, the Forfar one, and even the Dundee one. She respected her father's convinced faith: she was confirmed at St John's Church, Forfar. Increasingly, as her mother's health failed, she took over responsibility for the household.

In those four years of war she grew up, as the men she nursed had grown up. It meant that when she went back to London, and to society, she was even more her own person, with her own ideas and ideals. To the young Duke of York, newly-created in 1920, with serious health worries, concerned about industrial policy and social problems, she was, immediately, someone special. And she was. She was aware, even

Below: Lady Elizabeth, aged 9, on her pony, 'Bobs'.

Right: Lady Elizabeth and her sister, Lady Rose, welcome a soldier wounded in the 1914-1918 war to Glamis, which had been turned into a convalescent home for the duration of the war.

as the child of a wealthy family and a great house, of the peculiar, democratic thoughts and ways of the countryside she knew, of the hill and the river, and of the independent people who lived there and worked for her family. Nearby, in the mill towns, there was a liberal spirit and a Free Church one, and thrawn characters whom J.M. Barrie, from Kirriemuir, was putting in his plays. Hers happened to be an independent, not a deferential, community.

This was the second thing that mattered in her upbringing. She was used to people who talked back, had a good conceit of themselves, and judged the lairds and their children for what they were. Queen Victoria, coming upon the type on Deeside, on her Balmoral estate, had been entranced by it and, to her, its strangeness: so much so that she took John Brown as its exemplar. Lady Elizabeth knew it exactly for what it was, respected it, and knew how to cope with it. It was a good training. It was why she was different. Her husband-to-be, speaking in Glasgow immediately after the engagement, took credit for having, he said, 'the wisdom and good fortune to persuade a Scottish lady to share my life'.

It has evidently been no hindrance to the royal family to have had to guide it a woman who senses what plain people feel like, living in a political minority, whatever the minority may be. It has helped her, facing vociferous complaints about the English and their deeds

Right: The father of Lady Elizabeth, the Earl of Strathmore, and her older brother Lord Glamis, pictured here with her before her wedding.

through history, to say that she entirely understands and feels the same way. But it is also much more than that, and it is outside pleasantries and politics. A function of the Crown in a United Kingdom and in a Commonwealth of many nationalities, faiths and policies, is to help to unify and to encourage understanding. The Queen knows that better

Right: The Countess of Strathmore with her daughter, Lady Elizabeth, in 1930.

Top left: Glamis Castle.
Centre left: Balmoral Castle, rebuilt by Prince Albert in 1853-5.
Bottom left: On the Queen Mother's 80th birthday the royal family gave her the fishing hut shown here. The Queen Mother's response was 'some hut!'.
Top right: Birkhall, in the grounds of Balmoral. The Queen Mother took up residence here after the death of her husband.
Centre right: Balmoral was the Queen Mother's Scottish home until the death of King George VI.
Bottom right: Charlie Wright has been the Queen Mother's ghillie for 35 years. He is seen here fishing in the River Dee.

Right: The Queen Mother with Prince Charles at the Braemar Games, a favourite royal venue.

than anyone. The Queen Mother's instinct in these matters, too, comes from her roots.

She has, to this day, an official Scotland to which she is greatly attached. The Black Watch, of which she has been Colonel-in-Chief since time knows when, is one of her favourite regiments. Her husband was Lord High Commissioner to the General Assembly of the Church of Scotland in 1929, the first royal commissioner for centuries, in one of its most important years: the year of the reunion. She was with him, and with the united church, at Holyroodhouse. She chose to have her second child born at Glamis in August, 1930, still an occasion (as the child might be a boy and so higher than the Princess Elizabeth in the short line of succession) when it was thought a Home Secretary should be in near, if not exactly close, attendance. It was a stormy evening and the poor man was not happy. The tradition has now been dispensed with.

The baby was, of course, a girl, eventually called Margaret Rose (because the King vetoed the idea of Anne), the first royal child born in Scotland since 1602 – and the last, so far at least, since then.

There is, too, the unofficial Scotland in which she always senses she is at home. Naturally she went back to Glamis for part of her honeymoon and unromantically caught whooping cough; she has never been very expert at dealing with colds. She was loyal to Balmoral and its tradition, and was unhappy when she found Mrs Simpson briefly acting as hostess for Edward VIII there. She is still a pillar of support for the Braemar Highland games. But in many ways she has felt happier at Birkhall nearby, which is smaller and pleasanter and where the fishing is better. It was partly because she would be there from time to time that a young and dubious Prince Charles was encouraged to go off to school at Gordonstoun, to the north in Morayshire, and it was at Birkhall that she heard from her grandson of his early unhappy days there, sympathised with him, and insisted that he stick it out. She likes the tartan, and the pipes, and the strathspeys and reels at which she is expert and, her partners still say, inexhaustible.

In the end, she has given her energy and her heart to a smallish, once almost ruined castle on the north coast of Caithness, between Dunnet Head and Duncansby Head, and so at least as far north as John o' Groats ever lived: once called Barrogill, now the Castle of Mey. She found it, staying with friends, shortly after George VI's death. Sensibly,

Below left: The Castle of Mey. Restoring the Castle of Mey became a pre-occupation of the Queen Mother after the death of her husband. Here we see it in its present glory.
Below right: Despite the bitter winds blowing in from the north, the Queen Mother has managed to establish this beautiful garden by walling it in and creating a sun trap.

Below: On a misty, summer morning the Queen Mother had an open day for the Aberdeen Angus Society. The Queen Mother is well-known for her knowledge of livestock and on this page we see her inspecting cattle and some of her North Country Cheviot sheep. The bottom picture shows a young admirer offering the Queen Mother his toy binoculars.

realising that she felt, for the first time in years, she had nothing to put her hand to, they encouraged her to save it from decay and ruin. She has put a roof on it, restored it, furnished it and made it a home. She brought the neighbours in – and the family when they sail past in Britannia in the summer – and cultivated the garden against the cold and the wind. It was a labour of love for her. In a way, it came naturally to her. Just so had the lairds of her family worked to establish and restore their names and their estates. And so had she just done with the monarchy.

CHAPTER THREE

'The intolerable honour'

The reign of King George VI and Queen Elizabeth began under a deep shadow. It was cast by the departing, uncrowned Edward VIII. The new King had admired his elder brother and lived much of his life in awe of his charm, accomplishments and popularity. At the final dinner at Fort Belvedere in December, 1936, the then Duke of York had turned to Walter Monckton, Edward VIII's friend and adviser, and said: 'Look at him. We simply cannot let him go.' Edward was to recall that when he told the Duke he was abdicating he got no reply, his brother was 'so taken aback'. And the new King told Mountbatten: 'This is terrible, Dickie! I'm quite unprepared for it. David has been trained for it all his life, whereas I've never even seen a state paper.'

Whatever the Duke and Duchess of York had said to each other about Edward VIII's behaviour about Mrs Simpson, and his intentions towards her, the actual news, in the light of day, took them both by surprise. Returning from Scotland by the night train, they were faced with newspaper billboards proclaiming what up to then had been the unsayable in Fleet Street: 'The King's Marriage'. Those who were there

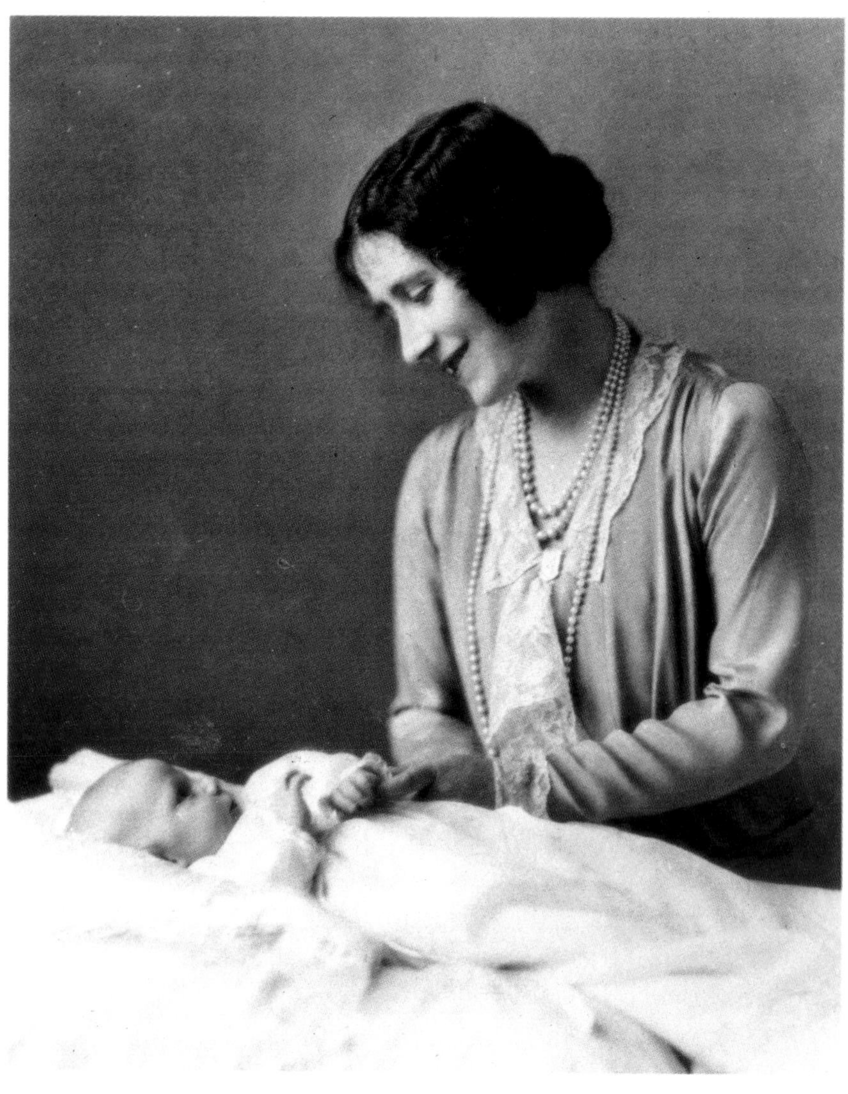

Right: The Duchess of York with the infant Princess Margaret Rose, 1930.

Right: The King and Queen with their daughters. The Queen is in 'Y Bwthyn Bach' (the Little House), gift of the people of Wales to the Princess Elizabeth.

noticed that for once the Duchess's smile failed her: she just patted her husband's hand. Plainly, they had not wanted it and felt themselves inadequate for it. She later called it 'the intolerable honour'. In truth, as the distraught Queen Mary said, 'the person who most needs sympathy is my second son. He is the one who is making the sacrifice'. The new Queen knew that; she already had her forebodings. Told that the Duchess of Windsor had stopped the Duke drinking, and that he no longer had pouches under his eyes, she asked, simply: 'Who has the pouches under his eyes now?'

What they had, and had strongly, was conscientiousness and a sense of duty. They were certainly needed. The Abdication was a crisis: Baldwin, the prime minister, carefully used the word himself. MPs spoke of controversy, grave difficulties and shock, and regularly of 'the constitutional issue', words that George V had spent his reign trying to steer away from the monarchy. The idea of Abdication was unknown to the British system: it was just not provided for in the Act of Settlement. Nor was Edward's half-idea of a morganatic marriage. All these novel thoughts, having been kept from the public for months, fell upon totally unready ears.

When the Commons debated the royal message of renunciation and on the next day, a Friday, the Abdication Bill itself, only seven Clydesiders divided the House in favour of a 'more stable and efficient form of government of a republican kind', but there was no mistaking

Right: A portrait of the Prince of Wales in 1925 by J. St Helier Lander. It is now in the City Art Gallery Leeds.

that even the committed royalists felt uneasy and let down. Maxton was naturally met by shouts of 'No' when he declared that 'the monarchical institution has now outlived its usefulness' because it was only a device, but Campbell Stephen frightened them by tackling head-on the monarchy's consistently-cultivated role as the link binding the Dominions and keeping the Empire together: 'If your Empire is being held together only by the weak link of monarchy, it is held by a very weak link.'

It was Major Attlee, the Labour leader, who made the two telling points that the new King and Queen, and their advisers, most needed to pay attention to. He had always favoured the monarchy (and would always do so) and he led his front bench in voting for the Bill, but, he said: 'I believe that a great disservice has been done to constitutional monarchy by over-emphasis and by vulgar adulation, particularly in the press.' That was one in the eye for the departing monarch. Second, he said, if constitutional monarchy were to survive, 'some pomp and ceremony may be useful on occasions, but we believe that the note of monarchy should be simplicity'. For that, he was talking to the right people. Their home life was essentially simple, their habits and, up to now, their means were relatively modest, their public reputation was unostentatious. They were prepared to work hard. But they were plainly untried and insecure. What seems to have worried them most was the departing king's reputation for easy popularity, and what he might get up to if and when he got bored with exile. At Balmoral Monckton talked to the new prime minister, Neville Chamberlain, and found he believed the Duke of Windsor should be given some royal functions, as if by the wave of a constitutional wand he had suddenly become a younger brother. But the Queen seems to have been adamant, whatever the King thought: 'I think the Queen felt quite plainly that it was undesirable to give the Duke any effective sphere of work . . . She naturally thought that she must be on her guard because the Duke of Windsor . . . might be the rallying point for any who might be critical of the new King, who was less superficially endowed with the arts and graces that please.' What the new team would have to be judged on was its own performance.

This, afterwards, may have seemed something of a misjudgment. In the last days before the Abdication the so-called King's Party had signally failed to rally effective popular support. Yet, on inexperienced and still impressionable young people, accustomed to the safe praise of politicians and press from their marriage onwards, the realisation dawned that a man like Churchill and papers like the *Express, Mail* and *News Chronicle* had actively encouraged Edward VIII to stay, and might not make matters exactly easy for them when the prodigal chose to return to the limelight. Churchill had declared that Edward would be 'particularly remembered in the homes of his poorer subjects'. Colonel Wedgwood had said MPs like him would take the oath of allegiance to the new King because the departing King wished it, and

Below left: The Daily Mirror, Tuesday December 8, 1936.
Below right: The Instrument of Abdication of Edward VIII, which was witnessed by his brother Albert, Duke of York, who succeeded him as King George VI.

THE DAILY MIRROR, Tuesday, December 8, 1936

Daily Mirror

GOD SAVE THE KING!

TUESDAY Dec. 8 No. 10303 ONE PENNY

MRS. SIMPSON READY TO GIVE UP THE KING

FROM OUR SPECIAL CORRESPONDENT

CANNES, Monday Night.

Mrs. Simpson is willing to give up the King if it would help to solve the present crisis.

But she does not think if she ended her friendship with him that it would help.

THAT is her statement delivered to-night officially by Lord Brownlow, Lord-in-Waiting to the King, on her behalf.

Lord Brownlow, accompanied by Mr. Herman Rogers, came to-night to the Hotel Majestic to give to more than twenty journalists from different countries an official statement from Mrs. Simpson.

The statement, which was read out by Lord Brownlow, is as follows :—

"Mrs. Simpson, throughout the last few weeks, has invariably wished to avoid any action or proposal which would hurt or damage his Majesty or the Throne.

"TO-DAY HER ATTITUDE IS UNCHANGED AND SHE IS WILLING, IF SUCH ACTION WOULD SOLVE THE PROBLEM, TO WITHDRAW FORTHWITH FROM A SITUATION WHICH HAS BEEN RENDERED BOTH UNHAPPY AND UNTENABLE."

Lord Brownlow read Mrs. Simpson's renunciation statement twice slowly to the assembled journalists.

STATEMENT SIGNED BY MRS. SIMPSON

Mr. Herman Rogers sat just behind him on the edge of the table. Neither would answer any questions nor make any addition to the statement.

They said they were making it on behalf of Mrs. Simpson and could not discuss it.

LORD BROWNLOW REFUSED TO SAY WHETHER THE STATEMENT HAD BEEN PREPARED WITH THE KNOWLEDGE OF KING EDWARD. ALL HE WOULD SAY WAS THAT IT WAS "AN OFFICIAL STATEMENT FROM MRS. SIMPSON," AND THAT SHE HERSELF HAD SIGNED IT.

Before he delivered the statement Lord Brownlow issued a denial. It read as follows:—

"Mrs. Simpson has given no interviews of any sort or kind, and made no statements to the Press whatsoever other than the statement I now make on her behalf."

Mrs. Simpson's Trunks Repacked, See Page 2.

Mrs. Simpson, who is willing, she says, to give up the King in order to ease the crisis.

BALDWIN CLEARS THE AIR

MR. Baldwin made a vital statement in the House of Commons last night which places the nation in possession of the facts.

His Majesty asked the Cabinet for their advice on the question of morganatic marriage—and on no other question. He wanted to know if it could be considered as a possible solution of the position in which he finds himself.

The Government have said that they are not prepared to introduce legislation to make such a marriage possible.

The Government have NOT said that they will not agree to marriage.

Already the Premier has stated that the King requires "no consent from any other authority to make his marriage legal."

The position, therefore, is this:—

The question of abdication need not arise.

The problem is clear—and now the decision rests with his Majesty.

It is neither necessary nor advisable for him to decide his course in haste. As Mr. Churchill has said, marriage can in no circumstances be accomplished for nearly five months.

And, it is understood too, that at no time has the suggestion been made that Mrs. Simpson should become Queen.

Weighing the Decision

MR. Attlee opened the question in Parliament yesterday by asking the Prime Minister whether he had anything to add to the statement he made on Friday.

Mr. Baldwin: "Yes, sir. I am glad to have the occasion of making a further statement on the position. In considering this whole matter it has always been, and remains, the earnest desire of the Government to afford to his Majesty the fullest opportunity of weighing a decision which involves so directly his own future happiness and the interests of all his subjects.

"At the same time, I cannot but be aware that any considerable prolongation of the present state of suspense and uncertainty would involve a risk of the greatest injury to national and Imperial interests.

"No one is more insistent on this aspect of the situation than his Majesty.

"In view of certain statements which have been made about relations between the Government and the King, I should add that, with the exception of the question of morganatic marriage, no advice has been tendered by the Government to his Majesty, with whom all my conversations have been strictly personal and informal.

"These matters were not raised first by the Government, but by his Majesty

(Continued on back page)

INSTRUMENT OF ABDICATION

I, Edward the Eighth, of Great Britain, Ireland, and the British Dominions beyond the Seas, King, Emperor of India, do hereby declare My irrevocable determination to renounce the Throne for Myself and for My descendants, and My desire that effect should be given to this Instrument of Abdication immediately.

In token whereof I have hereunto set My hand this tenth day of December, nineteen hundred and thirty six, in the presence of the witnesses whose signatures are subscribed.

SIGNED AT
FORT BELVEDERE
IN THE PRESENCE
OF

Edward R I

Albert

Henry

George

THE DAILY MIRROR, Saturday, December 12, 1936

Daily Mirror

No. 10307 — Registered at the G.P.O. as a newspaper. — ONE PENNY.

LONDON · ED ·

ROYAL FAMILY PARTY HEAR RADIO FAREWELL

The Son—and His Mother

I CAN'T GO ON WITHOUT THE WOMAN I LOVE

EX-KING Edward VIII broadcast to the world last night from the Augusta Tower of Windsor Castle. He was announced as his Royal Highness Prince Edward. He said:—

At long last I am able to say a few words of my own. I have never wanted to withhold anything. But until now it has not been constitutionally possible for me to speak.

A few hours ago I discharged my last duty as King and Emperor and now that I have been succeeded by my brother the Duke of York my first words must be to declare my allegiance to him. This I do with all my heart.

You all know the reasons which have impelled me to renounce the Throne, but I want you to understand that in making up my mind I did not forget the country, or the Empire which as Prince of Wales and later as King, I have for twenty-five years tried to serve; BUT YOU MUST BELIEVE ME WHEN I TELL YOU THAT I HAVE FOUND IT IMPOSSIBLE TO CARRY THE HEAVY BURDEN OF RESPONSIBILITY AND TO DISCHARGE MY DUTIES AS KING AS I WOULD WISH TO DO WITHOUT THE HELP AND SUPPORT OF THE WOMAN I LOVE. And I want you to know that the decision I have made has been mine, and mine alone.

This was a thing I had to judge entirely for myself. The other person most nearly concerned has tried up to the last to persuade me to take a different course. I have made this, the most serious decision of my life, only upon the single thought of what would in the end be best for all.

One Matchless Blessing

This decision has been made less difficult to me by the sure knowledge that my brother, with his long training in the public affairs of this country and with his fine qualities, was enabled to take my place forthwith without interruption or injury to the life and progress of the Empire.

And he has one matchless blessing, enjoyed by so many of you and not bestowed on me, a happy home with his wife and children.

During these hard days I have been comforted by her Majesty my mother and by my family. Ministers of the Crown, and in particular Mr. Baldwin the Prime Minister, have always treated me with full consideration.

There has never been any constitutional difference between me and them and between me and Parliament. Bred in the constitutional traditions of my father I should never have allowed any such issue to arise.

Ever since I was Prince of Wales and later on when I occupied the Throne I have been treated with the greatest kindness by all classes of the people wherever I have lived or journeyed throughout the Empire.

For that I am very grateful. I now quit altogether public affairs and I lay down my burden. It may be some time before I return to my native land but I shall always follow the fortunes of the British race and Empire with profound interest, and if at any time in the future I can be found of service to his Majesty in a private station, I shall not fail.

And [illegible] new King. I wish him and [illegible] people happiness and prosperity [illegible]

God bless [illegible]

GOD SAVE THE KING.

DISTRESS THAT IS FILLING MY HEART

A TOUCHING message to the nation and Empire, in which she refers to the "distress which fills a mother's heart," was issued by Queen Mary from Marlborough House last night. It read:—

To the people of this nation and Empire—

I have been so deeply touched by the sympathy which has surrounded me at this time of anxiety that I must send a message of gratitude from the depth of my heart.

The sympathy and affection which sustained me in my great sorrow less than a year ago have not failed me now, and are once again my strength and stay.

I NEED NOT SPEAK TO YOU OF THE DISTRESS WHICH FILLS A MOTHER'S HEART WHEN I THINK THAT MY DEAR SON HAS DEEMED IT TO BE HIS DUTY TO LAY DOWN HIS CHARGE, AND THAT THE REIGN WHICH HAD BEGUN WITH SO MUCH HOPE AND PROMISE HAS SO SUDDENLY ENDED.

I know that you will realise what it has cost him to come to this decision; and that, remembering the years in which he tried so eagerly to serve and help his country and Empire, you will ever keep a grateful remembrance of him in your hearts.

I COMMEND TO YOU HIS BROTHER, SUMMONED SO UNEXPECTEDLY AND IN CIRCUMSTANCES SO PAINFUL TO TAKE HIS PLACE. I ASK YOU TO GIVE TO HIM THE SAME FULL MEASURE OF GENEROUS LOYALTY WHICH YOU GAVE TO MY BELOVED HUSBAND, AND WHICH YOU WOULD WILLINGLY HAVE CONTINUED TO GIVE TO HIS BROTHER.

With him I commend my dear daughter-in-law, who will be his Queen. May she receive the same unfailing affection and trust which you have given to me for six and twenty years. I know that you have already taken her children to your hearts.

IT IS MY EARNEST PRAYER THAT, IN SPITE OF, NAY THROUGH, THIS PRESENT TROUBLE, THE LOYALTY AND UNITY OF OUR LAND AND EMPIRE MAY BY GOD'S BLESSING BE MAINTAINED AND STRENGTHENED. MAY HE BLESS AND KEEP AND GUIDE YOU ALWAYS. MARY R.

EX-KING'S EMOTION

With tears in his voice as he spoke of "the woman I love," Mr. Windsor, ex-King Edward VIII, bade farewell to the Empire last night.

THE whole world listened to his speech. Scores of millions heard the break in his voice as he said, "God bless you all," and the inspiring, ringing tones as he uttered the final:

"GOD SAVE THE KING."

For nine minutes the tragic story of a King's love—a love without which he had found it impossible to carry on—held the world spellbound.

The broadcast was made from Windsor Castle. The title used in introducing him—"His Royal Highness Prince Edward"—was purely a courtesy of the B.B.C. the *Daily Mirror* was informed.

For the present the ex-King has no titles, and is simply "Mr. Edward Windsor."

After the broadcast he motored back to Royal Lodge, Windsor, arriving at 10.20.

Family Party

At the lodge where they had earlier gathered for a farewell dinner-party were the Royal Family.

The guests were the new King, the ex-King, Queen Mary, the Duke of Gloucester, the Princess Royal, Princess Alice and the Earl of Athlone.

It was a typical family gathering with those

(Continued on back page)

KING GEORGE VI ACKNOWLEDGING CHEERS AS HE AND THE DUKE OF GLOUCESTER LEFT 145, PICCADILLY, FOR WINDSOR TO JOIN OTHER MEMBERS OF THE ROYAL FAMILY IN THE FAREWELL DINNER AT ROYAL LODGE.

THE DAILY MIRROR, Friday, December 11, 1936

No. 10306 — Registered at the G.P.O. as a newspaper. — ONE PENNY

EDWARD VIII WILL BROADCAST TO-NIGHT AS PRIVATE CITIZEN

Britain's new King and Queen, the Duke and Duchess of York. Their elder daughter, Princess Elizabeth, now ten years old, is heir to the Throne.

Picture pages are 8, 12, 14, 16, 17, 19 and 28.

Edward VIII will broadcast to the Empire and the world to-night as a "private individual owing allegiance to the new King."

This will follow the signing of his abdication papers and the succession to the Throne of his brother, the Duke of York, who will be 41 on Monday.

The time has been fixed tentatively for 10 p.m.

EDWARD VIII's DESIRE TO SPEAK TO HIS PEOPLES DID NOT REACH THE B.B.C. UNTIL LATE LAST NIGHT. AT ONCE ARRANGEMENTS WERE MADE FOR THE MOST DRAMATIC BROADCAST THAT THE CORPORATION HAS EVER BEEN CALLED UPON TO HANDLE TO BE RELAYED TO ALL PARTS OF THE WORLD.

He may broadcast from Fort Belvedere, when it would be his last act on British soil before he goes abroad. Should he leave the country earlier in the evening, arrangements will be made for him to speak from abroad.

When his voice is heard to-night Edward VIII may, according to one belief, have become plain Mr. Edward Windsor.

Britain's new King, the Duke of York, some believe, may take the title of King George VI instead of Albert I. His wife will become Queen at thirty-six.

The two brothers dined together at Fort Belvedere last night and at a late hour were still occupied with State papers and official documents.

On returning to his home just before midnight the Duke's car was mobbed and took some minutes to drive the last few yards into the forecourt of the house.

The great multitude stood outside and sang the National Anthem, "For He's a Jolly Good Fellow," and chanted in unison "We want our King and Queen."

EMPIRE HEARS NEWS WITH UTMOST CALM

The dramatic announcement of abdication made in the House of Commons yesterday was received with the utmost calm throughout the Empire.

In London the vast crowds which gathered in Whitehall, Downing-street and Piccadilly, last night, were comparatively quiet save for demonstrations by a few hooligans.

They sang "God Save the King!" they sang "For He's a Jolly Good Fellow!" they shouted "We Want King Albert!"

A man with a megaphone marched at the head of a party which came along the Mall, shouting "Long Live King Albert!"

Crowds gathered near Downing-street too last night. At ten o'clock the little street was cleared and a cordon of police guarded the Whitehall entrance.

Three minutes later several hundred Fascists came running down Whitehall from Trafalgar-square, shouting at the top of their voices and brandishing newspapers.

(Continued on back page)

News of the Abdication dominated the front pages of the papers.

'if they sometimes raise their glass to the King across the water, who shall blame them?' Another MP spoke of the 'understanding, the sympathy and the good will' Edward had always had among ex-service men. These reminders of what the country genuinely thought it was missing were not meant to be hurtful, but, as they were what the new King himself believed, they were not especially comforting. It was a natural enough feeling at the time. Even in 1940 George VI may have felt slightly more inclined to welcome Halifax as a coalition prime minister than Churchill; though that reservation quickly disappeared. What would have made it impossible for the Windsors to take up any sort of active royal life was the presence of the new Duchess herself, whom both the Queen and Queen Mary had indicated they would never receive. But if the new team were to be judged by results, and would judge themselves by them, what, in fact, was it up against? It was true that Edward VIII had tried to modernise the monarchy himself, as his long experience under his father's thumb had taught him was overdue. What he wanted had support, but the way he tried to do it revealed within months his chronic inadequacies and his own sense of them. Of all George V's sons, he was the one who had stood up to him, and had earned the respect of the rest of the family. They, like the country, believed that he represented a new start. It was the Duke and Duchess of York who learned at first hand that he was not up to it, that Mrs Simpson had become the be-all, and would, if he were not sensible, become the end-all, of his reign.

He had wanted to rationalise the work of the royal palaces and reduce their staffs. But he had no idea of how to go about it. He cut back drastically at Balmoral without even thinking of consulting his brother and sister-in-law at Birkhall, though they had a proper, practical sense of what could be done. It was the Duke of York who had to open Aberdeen's new hospital buildings in September, 1936, though the King, who had been asked, gave public priority to meeting Mrs Simpson off the train at Ballater that day. Edward resolved to clear out all the officials around him who had been George V's men; as a result he had few whom he felt he could trust when the time came to risk the matter of his marriage.

He liked to think of himself as an innovator, but could not quite bring himself to innovate. He disliked taking the declaration to uphold the Protestant faith, but decided not to make it an issue. Apart from that, his abiding memory of his only state opening of Parliament was the smell of mothballs from the peers' robes. He was bored to tears by much of the court routine and did not bother to conceal it: the day he left the debutantes unintroduced and out in the rain in Buckingham Palace garden may have been a small step towards modernity but it seemed merely puerile. If anything, it made his successors too anxious not to break with the past.

The truth was that in everything serious that Edward VIII turned his hand to, his brother could already do better, and his wife knew it. There was only one political issue in Edward's brief reign – and he was it. He had seen his conservative father having to agree with the reform of the House of Lords, the extension of the franchise to universal male, and then female, suffrage, and the arrival of the first Labour government. But Edward was interested in only one question of state: his own marriage. There was another issue, unemployment, which did appeal to his better feelings and which, subsequently, was used by his defenders to explain both his true nature and why the Baldwin government wanted to be rid of him. Yet even that was not what popular recollection made it out to be.

Below: The Duke and Duchess of Windsor returned to England on June 7, 1967 for the unveiling of a plaque to Queen Mary at Marlborough House. The couple are here greeted by the Queen Mother.

Right: An early portrait of the new Queen Consort from the Illustrated London News, May 15, 1937.

Edward's tour of South Wales, where he said 'Something must be done to find them work,' and 'You may be sure that all I can do for you I will', took place only three weeks before he abdicated and left the country. By contrast, the Duke of York's interest in industrial relations, which had amused his brothers, had been evident since his time at Cambridge where he read economics and civics. He supported the Industrial Welfare Society, and began – what royalty seldom did then – visiting factories. When he married, his wife backed him up and went with him through the depressed areas. They had seen for themselves. From his own pocket he paid for summer camps at which boys from public schools met boys from the slums. This concern was not forgotten when he came to the throne.

It was Edward who started the King's Flight, now the Queen's Flight. It was another sign that here was a king who really was up with the times. He got the Air Ministry to take over the plane's maintenance and the salaries of the pilot and mechanics. Yet he then used it to ferry his friends as he liked and even to bring in goods on which duty should have been paid. But it was his brother who was the real airman. He went to Cranwell and got his wings in 1919; the only British sovereign, so far, to have qualified. He even wore RAF uniform at his wedding. That the Yorks should have felt in the grip of such an inferiority complex in December, 1936, seems remarkable. But they did.

There was another constraint. Some echelons of society had affected

Right: King George VI as seen in the same issue of the Illustrated London News.

not to know who the Yorks were anyway. Just 10 months before the Abdication, Harold Nicolson, the National Labour MP and former diplomat, married to Vita Sackville-West, wrote to her describing an evening at which, 'when I got in, there was a dear little woman in black sitting on the sofa, and she said to me, "We have not met since Berlin."' He could not place her at all (although most of the country, going to the cinema and reading the picture papers, would have found no difficulty) until, as he put it, 'another woman came in and curtsied low to her and I realised it was the Duchess of York.' That would not have helped confidence, even though, just over a year later, he wrote eulogistically in his diary that at a palace dinner 'nothing could exceed the charm or dignity which she displays, and I cannot help feeling what a mess poor Mrs Simpson would have made of such an occasion'. But that was later indeed.

Even Baldwin had a certain patronising nonchalance about the monarchy which his public speeches never quite revealed. Asked in the Commons lobby about what the plans were for the coronation of George VI and Queen Elizabeth, he said they would keep to the day long planned for Edward VIII: 'Same day. New king.' Baldwin had been at his best during the Abdication crisis, and he knew it. He was not to go out a beleagured figure, harried over rearmament and the economy, after all. He would retire with the accumulated credit he thought he deserved. At the coronation it was noticed that he received

Left and right: The Crowning of the King and the Queen Consort on May 12, 1937.

the loyal cheers as if they were equally meant for him. Baldwin and Chamberlain: neither was precisely the man to give young people confidence in a difficult part as Melbourne once gave Victoria and Churchill later hoped to give Elizabeth II.

In December, 1936, there was nothing for it but to be true to themselves. The new King spoke no more than the truth when he told his Accession Council, 'with my wife and helpmeet by my side I take up the heavy task which lies before me'. They were partners. He immediately gave her the Garter. Sensibly, they restored the seasoned advisers who had incurred Edward's displeasure. They took up every public engagement possible, the King insisting that he would go to South Wales: 'Where my brother went I will go too.' The Princesses were, as they had always been, a focus of friendly attention. Queen Mary gave loyal support, especially over the prospective Duchess of Windsor. By May 12, 1937, they and the country were ready for the coronation.

On the day it rained. The London busmen were out on strike. A Presbyterian chaplain fainted in the procession. There were fumbles. The crown went on precariously. A bishop stood on the King's robe

Opposite: Queen Elizabeth photographed by Cecil Beaton in Buckingham Palace, 1939.

and had to be told to 'get off it pretty smartly'. These things happen at most coronations. The previous one had been 26 years before, so not everyone knew quite what they were doing all the time. But the King spoke well in his responses: that had been another ordeal because the patronising Archbishop of Canterbury had seen fit to warn the country that the King had a stammer and they should bear with him. No wonder the King and Queen could not sleep: they woke at three am. The King could not eat any breakfast. The Queen, faithful to old friends, had not gone to any stylish new couturier for her robe or dress but to her old court dressmaker. But she did admirably: 'the little Queen advanced with a real poetry of motion', as the Archbishop observed. She was poised and apparently serene as she was anointed and crowned, and then took her place on her throne beside her husband's. When they got back to the palace she was overcome with exhaustion and had almost lost her voice. She went straight to bed.

It had been a triumph. It was so because the King and Queen had already shown their dedication; people believed in them. It was so because Queen Mary arrived, the first time a Queen Mother had attended the coronation of her successor – and because the two Princesses were there, wearing junior versions of Queen Mary's robe. It was so, above all, because the country willed it to be so. Whatever Attlee might have thought and had to forgive, there was adulation and a great deal of it. The service was broadcast around the world by radio. The BBC's new television cameras were refused entry to Westminster Abbey, as they very nearly were even for the coronation in 1953, and had to put up with a place on the route. It was a novelty. The film cameras had a field day. In many ways it was to be their finest ceremonial hour, and cinema audiences applauded the special colour pictures when they came on. It was, too, the heyday of the illustrated magazines, glossy and rotogravure, bought and kept as souvenirs. All the newspapers, naturally, had their own picture supplements. There was no longer any doubt of who now had the country's loyalty and affection.

It was the manifestation of a national wish, if not exactly to start again, then still to look for hope in a darkening world. The Berlin-Rome axis had been formed. Spain was torn by civil war. Japan had invaded China. For the next two years the British government was to try every recourse to avoid fighting: delusion and self-deception had to be maintained, even in royal utterances. Launching the Queen Elizabeth at Clydebank in September, 1938, the Queen read out a message from the King: 'He bids the people of this country to be of good cheer, in spite of the dark clouds hanging over them, and indeed over the whole world.' That very night Chamberlain told the Czech government to accept Hitler's occupation terms and went on the radio to tell Britain: 'How horrible, fantastic, incredible it is that we should be digging trenches and trying on gas-masks here because of a quarrel in a far-away country between people of whom we know nothing.'

By the next summer there were few doubts left, even in the government. The royal visit to Canada and the United States in May, 1939, had a serious diplomatic purpose, When the war came it would be essential to have North America firmly on the Allied side. There were few doubts about Canada, but the United States was evidently both harder to persuade and much more essential. No king had visited before: George III had never appreciated the value of royal tours.

Above: The Queen Consort in the gardens of Buckingham Palace, 1939. Another in the sequence of Cecil Beaton photographs.

A celebrated mayor of Chicago had once won election by threatening to punch the King of England on the nose. But the King and Queen were welcomed with calculated charm by President Roosevelt. He, too, understood the necessity of demonstrating the natural alliance between the two great English-speaking democracies which had been a matter of practical diplomatic policy for most of the century but which would again need to have American opinion brought squarely behind it before the United States could play its full part against the dictatorships.

All had been arranged. But as the King and Queen set sail for Canada, the Duke of Windsor happened to broadcast a very different message to the United States (on NBC) from Verdun, the scene of daily carnage in the Great War. The setting was highly evocative to the French who had fought there and to British ex-service men who had taken terrible casualties further north to help the French. His appeal was pitched specifically for peace and reconciliation with the Germans. It may have been, in part at least, deliberate; it was, more probably, thoughtless. Afterwards, when the war had been fought, he said lightly: 'I thought we could be fence-sitters while the Nazis and the Reds slugged it out.' Whatever it was meant to be, it was felt at the time that it could, at a stroke, have jeopardised the royal visit. It did not. The Roosevelts played their part: they decided the young couple had a rare capacity for making friends. The crowds felt the same. The return to London was marked by admiration that went beyond the customary thanks for a successful royal tour. But by then Hitler had already decided that he could take Poland, and no one could stop him.

The King and Queen developed a country lifestyle at Sandringham House. The two top pictures in this sequence show the King and Queen going to meet their guests at a garden party and Queen Elizabeth chatting with the local ladies.
The Queen Mother has come to Sandringham every July in her widowhood. The two central pictures show Sandringham House as it is today and the Queen Mother receiving a gift of flowers at the Sandringham Show. The picture bottom left shows a young well-wisher with a present which is rather larger than herself. The panda got a seat of honour when the Queen Mother left the Show.

CHAPTER FOUR

'I shall not go down'

The war that began on September 3, 1939, was the test of the country, and of the convalescent monarchy. There was nothing easy, at the time, in giving comfort and encouragement to a country that was, in the summer of 1940, plainly losing. It was no more in Queen Elizabeth's mind to be a loser than it was in most of her people's. As the monarchs of Norway and the Netherlands fled to London and those of Belgium and Denmark became prisoners in their own country, and as France fell to defeat and capitulation in June, 1940, the Queen told Harold Nicolson that she was being taught every morning how to fire a revolver. 'Yes,' she said, 'I shall not go down like the others.'

It was the bombing that brought London, and the country, nearest to going down. When the German attacks on the south of England airfields had narrowly failed to turn the Battle of Britain, the bombers went for London: at first the East End especially. The blitz that duly began on September 7, 1940, continued for the next fifty-seven successive nights and was not stopped until May, 1941; 20,000 civilians were killed and 70,000 wounded. Not only were the defences inadequate to stop night bombing, the deep shelters in London were found to be hopelessly insufficient, overcrowded and insanitary. The

Opposite: The King and Queen inspect bomb damage during the war. Their own home, Buckingham Palace, received several direct hits. Below: King George and Queen Elizabeth visiting ARP units during the Second World War.

public were ordered not to sleep in the tube stations, but 200,000 people a night simply went down there and refused to come out. Morale was ebbing away. Communists circulated peace petitions in the shelters. George Orwell wrote darkly in his diary that he was reminded of St Petersburg on the eve of the revolution.

Early that September, as the King and Queen went to the destroyed areas in the East End, there were reports of booing. There was resentment that the bombs always seemed to fall there, near the docks, the first target as the bombers' navigators found their way up the Thames in darkness. Then the attacks spread westwards. On September 13, a bold Luftwaffe pilot, under cover of the rain clouds, flew straight up the Mall and dropped six bombs on Buckingham Palace. Two exploded in the quadrangle as the King and Queen watched from an upstairs sitting room thirty yards away. Immediately afterwards, they went back to the East End and were loudly cheered. It was then that the Queen made her most memorable remark of the war: 'I'm glad we've been bombed. It makes me feel I can look the East End in the face.' London showed it could take it. By October a Londoner, Herbert Morrison, had been made Home Secretary and Minister of Home Security; and by then, too, there was a marked reluctance to be sent to any air raid shelter near the palace. The palace was hit nine times in all.

As the raids spread to all the great cities that winter, the job of being there the day after to encourage the firemen and the rescuers, to

Below: In August 1941 the Royal couple visited the East End of London, where their concern was greatly appreciated by the people.

Right: A charming study of the Princesses Elizabeth and Margaret with their mother, Queen Elizabeth, taking lessons in the garden at Windsor in 1941.

console the mourning and cheer up the injured, became increasingly important. The royal train of three carriages moved about the country, stopping in obscure sidings at night. The Queen herself organised lorries to take supplies and practical help to the worst-hit. And, never in uniform, a civilian among civilians, she went round the bombed streets, clambering over the debris. In all her public appearances since, on high days and holidays, however splendid or simple the ceremony, there are those of her generation who will never forget what she faced and did then.

She was good with the evacuees, and with the families who took them in and needed to be persuaded it was worthwhile. She had an exemplary way with her at military hospitals; her years at Glamis in the Great War helped her there. She could encourage allotment holders, happily growing their own vegetables for the war effort. She even tried to have a good word for the Ministry of Food's recipes. Eleanor Roosevelt, staying in a draughty, unheated Buckingham Palace in 1942, found the baths painted with a Plimsoll line to save hot water, and the King and Queen carefully eating their own wartime rations, as they always did, although they were served, in the visitor's honour, on gold and silver plates.

Above: The King and Queen consoling people made homeless by the bombing in Sheffield in 1941.

These were the years when she knew her speeches would really matter, and when the radio, the most powerful propaganda weapon of all, must be used to the very best advantage. She broadcast to the women of occupied France with understanding and hope. In 1941, with the United States not yet in the war, she spoke directly to the Americans to thank them for the aid, the 'bundles for Britain' that went straight to those who had been hit in the Blitz. She told them what the women of Britain were doing: serving in the armed forces, in the land army, in the civil service, driving lorries and ambulances, and the nurses who 'in the black horror of a bombed hospital, never falter and, though often wounded, think always of their patients and never of themselves'.

But, she said, 'wherever I go I see bright eyes and smiling faces, for though our road is stony and hard, it is straight, and we know that we fight in a great cause'.

Her task, as she saw it, was to ensure that, in the country that was the most fully mobilised of all the powers, women played their essential part not only in the services and factories but in the home – and were honoured for it. She knew the uncertainties and worries and could express them and sympathise with them. When victory was at last in sight at the end of 1944 she told civil defence workers in London: 'I believe strongly that when future generations look back on this most terrible war, they will recognise as one of its chief features the degree to which women were actively concerned in it. I do not think it is any exaggeration to say that in this country, at any rate, the war could not have been won without their help.' Instilling that pride was her biggest contribution.

She had her own anxieties like everyone else. There was the safety of the two Princesses. It was suggested they might be better off in Canada, away from the bombs and any attempted invasion. The Queen quickly settled that in a famous formula: they would not leave her, she would not leave the King, and the King would never leave. So the Princesses spent much of the war getting their education behind the walls of Windsor Castle, until Princess Elizabeth got her father to agree to her joining the ATS, where she was a junior transport officer and proudly learned to drive heavy lorries. 'We had sparking plugs all last night at dinner', her mother said.

There was, too, the more intractable problem of the in-laws, the Windsors. The Queen had had no truck at all with the Windsors' political and social flirtation with the Nazis, however harmless it was

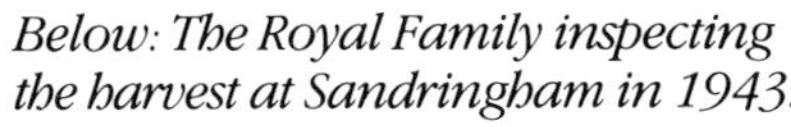

Below: The Royal Family inspecting the harvest at Sandringham in 1943.

all said to be. It added to her feeling about the Duke's desertion from the crown and about the Duchess who had encouraged him to do it.

She saw no reason why in 1939, with the King now plainly succeeding in becoming the symbol of loyalty in a united nation, the former king should be allowed back at the centre of the war effort attempting to live down his own unpopularity. The Duke was sent off back to France again to exercise his talents in the military mission in Paris.

That ended with the German advance, and the Windsors' swift and unheroic exit to fascist Spain. The Duke lingered in Madrid, if not in hope of anything substantial from the Germans, then, at least, negotiating petulantly with London for a senior war job and for the title 'royal highness' for his wife. Both were denied him again. He waited in Lisbon, worrying about getting his furniture out of occupied Paris, while the Duchess was especially distraught at the loss of her favourite bathing costume and got the American embassy to rescue it for her from Antibes. The German foreign minister, von Ribbentrop, believed now that something useful could be made of the Windsors; after all, Hitler himself had said, on meeting the Duchess in 1937: 'She would have made a good queen.' Frau Goring had thought the same. As word of the Windsors' ambivalence and dilatoriness filtered back to London and to a government and royal family mobilising for a decisive battle, it was essential that not too much of this should get out to the country. In the end the Duke gave in to good sense: he and his wife departed to govern the Bahamas. They had no sympathisers left. The doubts that the King and Queen had entertained about them were seen to be vindicated.

In August, 1942, the news came that the youngest of the brothers, the Duke of Kent, an air commodore in the RAF, had been killed on active service. His son, Prince Michael, had been christened at Windsor just a month before, and the Duke had looked in to see the King and Queen at Balmoral before setting off to inspect the British bases in Iceland. Thirty minutes airborne and in bad weather, the plane crashed on a mountainside near Dunbeath, in Caithness. The King felt this loss most deeply. He said he felt he was about to break down at the funeral service at Windsor. He did not rest until he had gone himself to see the spot where his brother had died. The news had come to them in the quiet of Deeside, where they were having a brief holiday: it was precisely the sort of news that telegrams took daily to an increasing number of homes.

What the Queen saw was the strain that the war was increasingly putting on her husband's health. Like her, he had worked tirelessly, but he did not have her resilience. Even so, he was concerned to get Churchill's approval to go to see his armies abroad. In June, 1943, he flew to Gibraltar and on to North Africa. She was worried. There was news of fog but none of the plane. She wrote to Queen Mary: 'Complete silence till a few minutes ago, when a message came that they have landed in Africa and taken off again. Of course I imagined every sort of horror, and walked up and down my room staring at the telephone.'

These nerves were never seen in public. In the King's absence she carried on, as she expected others to do. As a Counsellor of State she held an investiture at the palace, the first one to be held by a queen since Victoria's day. The Dambusters, the men who had broken the

Moehne and Eder dams, were among those she decorated: the VC going to Wing-Commander Guy Gibson. She understood, even when she was worried about her husband's wish to see some of the fighting, and did not try to veto his plan to sail across the Channel to Normandy on D-Day. That was vetoed for her.

When victory came in Europe the Buckingham Palace balcony was opened for the first time since the war began. King, Queen and Princesses came out with Churchill. The family were called back seven times more by crowds that had lived for that hour. The King's thoughts were for his daughters: the poor dears, he thought, had never had any fun, so let them go off into the celebrating throng. But she could tell now that he was utterely exhausted, as indeed she was for the moment herself. He admitted he was 'burnt out'. He had fewer than seven years left to live, increasingly punctuated by illness and painful operations, and by more anxiety – this time about the economic recovery of the country.

It seemed that theirs was not to be a reign for easy times. For them success, admiration, affection merely led on to new challenges and problems. For her, watching his slow, brave decline, there can often have been the thought that she was nursing the last casualty of the war.

Below: V.E. Day, May 8, 1945. The Royal Family on the balcony of Buckingham Palace with the Prime Minister, Winston Churchill.

CHAPTER FIVE

The Austerity Monarchy

The peace brought its own problems for her: after the wartime monarchy, the austerity monarchy. In one sense the war had even been easier: everyone in Britain had been on the same side. Now, in a country where rationing became even stricter in peacetime, where there was so much damage to be made good, and which was surviving on American and Canadian loans that soon ran down, party politics added rancour to the disappointment that victory had not brought in a brave new world. It was immediately evident that there could be no early return to the court ceremonial of pre-war days. What the Attlee government wanted of the palace was simplicity indeed. Everything would have to take its turn, even repairs to the palace itself. An expensive monarchy, with the old glitter and trappings, was not the official mood of the country. On the left, it became fashionable again to talk about the bicycling monarchies of Scandinavia and the Netherlands. A royal family without a touch of glamour might be hardworking and helpful but it did not seem a particularly useful job.

That was changed by Princess Elizabeth. She was in love. It had been the worst winter imaginable. Snow lay over much of the country until

In 1947 the King and Queen sailed to South Africa with their daughters. Top left shows them receiving a last farewell from Queen Mary and the Duchess of Kent.
Top right: The Royal Family on board H.M.S. Vanguard.
Bottom left: A radiant Queen Elizabeth enjoying the sea breeze.
Bottom right: Table Mountain looms in the background as the Royal Family leave South Africa.

April. The coal ran out, industry went on short time, and unemployment rose briefly to 4.5 million. Then, on July 10, 1947, came the announcement: 'It is with the greatest pleasure that the King and Queen announce the betrothal of their dearly beloved daughter, the Princess Elizabeth, to Lieutenant Philip Mountbatten, RN . . . to which union the King has gladly given his consent.' The title of the bridegroom to be was immediately improved to a dukedom. And at least half the country felt it had something to look forward to at last.

It was the Queen who organised things, remembering her own wedding at the Abbey twenty-four years before. First, there was the problem of clothes rationing: it would not be seemly for a royal wedding to break the regulations. The bride was allowed a hundred coupons for herself and twenty-five for each of the bridesmaids. No one need have worried: the loyal public sent in its coupons to make sure the Princess had a proper gown and trousseau. Then there was the procession: for once the rules were relaxed. Through the streets of London on November 20th went the Irish state coach for the first time since 1939, and riding with it were the Household Cavalry, back in their real uniform at last. It was said to be one of the biggest royal gatherings of the century. The crowds who were there and the rest of the population who saw it all on the cinema newsreels had a glimpse of what they had been missing. If it seemed no more than what Bagehot called 'a pretty event', it was all part of the necessary business of cheering the country up.

The King and Queen, proud of their eldest daughter as they were, did have a real sense of loss. Because theirs had been such a close family, and in the war having to rely so much on each other for company and comfort and entertainment, they could not have felt otherwise. The King himself put it in a letter to the Princess: 'Our family, us four, the 'Royal Family' must remain together with additions of course at suitable moments!! I have watched you grow up all these years with pride under the skilful direction of Mummy, who as you know is the most marvellous person in the world in my eyes . . .' The

Right: The King and Queen at the wedding of their eldest daughter, Princess Elizabeth to Prince Philip, Duke of Edinburgh, Nov. 20, 1947.

Queen herself said to a friend: 'What a wonderful day it has been. They grow up and leave us, and we must make the best of it.'

She did. Next April there was their silver wedding to celebrate, and the country insisted on celebrating with them. Out came the state landau and the Household Cavalry again for the drive to St Paul's. The Archbishop of Canterbury said it for everyone: 'The nation and the empire bless God that He has set such a family at the seat of our royalty.' That evening, on the radio, the Queen declared her conviction that the sanctities of married life provided a rock-like foundation on which all the best in the life of the nation was built. 'Looking back over the last 25 years and to my own happy childhood I realise more and more that wonderful sense of security and happiness which comes from a loved home.' That November her first grandson, Prince Charles, was born.

But that same month there was bad news. The King, long a heavy smoker, had been suffering increasingly from cramps in his legs: smoking had caused the degeneration of his arteries. The doctors said bluntly that there was a possibility of gangrene and a foot might even have to be amputated. He did have an operation in March, 1949, and a lengthy rest seemed to do him good. Tours abroad had to be cancelled. The Queen took on many of his public appearances. Princess Anne's birth in August, 1950, did cheer him up, and he was there for the opening of the Festival of Britain on the South Bank in the summer of 1951, wryly noticing that its centrepiece and symbol, the skylon, was 'virtually unsupported, like the economy'. All the time she saw the signs of his growing weariness and depression. That autumn she was told, although he was not, that he had cancer of the lung.

There was nothing she could do then but wait, and help him as she had always done. That winter his Christmas broadcast to the country and Commonwealth had to be recorded line by line: his voice could not have done it otherwise. On January 31, 1952, he went, plainly frail and finely drawn, to see his daughter and son-in-law off on their way to Kenya, at the start of the royal tour of Australia that he was no longer well enough to undertake. There was still hope that he would see them return. Back at Sandringham, where he had been born, he enjoyed a day's shooting, wearing a specially heated waistcoat. That night he went early to bed, and a servant brought him cocoa at eleven pm. At midnight a watchman outside saw him close his window. When they came to rouse him in the morning he was dead. He was only fifty-six.

For her, who had known to expect it, it was still a sacrifice that she felt he should never have been asked to make. They had not wanted the throne. They had worked to restore the reputation of the monarchy in difficult years, when criticism and cynicism would have fastened on any mistake. They had helped to see the country through the most perilous of all its modern wars. They had, no less, been of signal importance in the years of the disappointing peace. Now a reign of so much achievement had been cut short; the man who had done so much for the country had given his life.

There followed the sad procession from Sandringham House to the church nearby, where the dead King lay like a country squire, watched over by his estate servants. Then the journey by train to London, as his father had gone sixteen years before. Then the lying-in-state in

Previous page: The King and Queen with their younger daughter, Princess Margaret, on her 21st birthday.

Westminster Hall, where over 300,000 of his subjects filed past in a last offering of respect to their ruler and friend. The Duke of Windsor came himself with Queen Mary. And then the final interment at St George's, Windsor. Few kings have been so genuinely mourned. Few, if any, have been remembered publicly as having reigned so much in partnership with their wife; and none would have acknowledged it as openly as he always did.

The Times noticed something more. 'When history comes to be written,' it said, 'it may be held not the least of the debts this country owes to her that she maintained personal oversight in every detail of the education of the Heiress-Presumptive. It was not a bookish education, nor one that followed any of the 'advanced' experimental theories of the day, but it was calculated to keep the princess's mind receptive, her interests wide and sensitive, her appreciation of nature

Below: The King and Queen at London Airport bid farewell to Princess Elizabeth and the Duke of Edinburgh setting out for Nairobi. One week later the King died and Princess Elizabeth returned to England as Queen.

Above: The heavily veiled figures of the Royal ladies attending the funeral service of King George VI.

and the arts lively, and above all her heart simple and open to human things.'

That was the prescription for the new monarchy, and there was no doubt where the credit lay. Of the Queen Mother herself: 'Her birth and upbringing were British and outside the old society in which kings have married . . . The barrier that had, in the past, often kept royalty from everyday contact and easy acquaintance with other people, went down before the social charm and the wide range of friendships of the Queen Mother.'

So it had ended. The coffin had lain in St George's heaped with flowers. Garter King-of-Arms recited over the grave the roll of titles of the dead sovereign and of the new. To the country the Queen Mother sent a special message: 'He loved you all, every one of you, most truly. That, you know, was what he always tried to tell you in his yearly message at Christmas. Throughout our married life we have tried, the King and I, to fulfil with all our hearts and all our strength the great task of service that was laid upon us. My only wish now is that I may be allowed to continue the work that we sought to do together.

'I commend to you our dear daughter. Give her your loyalty and devotion: in the great and lonely station to which she has been called she will need your protection and your love.'

Overleaf: The Royal Family group photograph taken at Buckingham Palace on the occasion of the Coronation of Queen Elizabeth II in June 1953.

The picture that remained in the country's mind had been of the three queens, Queen Mary, Queen Elizabeth and the new Queen, all dressed in black. To them went sympathy, affection, and a recognition, conscious and unconscious, of just how much the nation had lost.

CHAPTER SIX

'Isn't it exciting!'

She has always travelled well. Long before she became an international phenomenon and diplomatic asset, she seemed to know by instinct how to appeal to the crowds: recognising their friendship without ever courting them. At the start it was said to be her eyes, large, blue eyes looking out from under a twenties hair-do or an off-the-forehead hat of the kind that she wore from the beginning deliberately because it gave the people who had come miles to see her the chance to see her properly. They thought of her then as 'the little Duchess' already in an affectionate and proprietorial way, though she may not always have appreciated the attention to her height: she stands five-feet two-inches without her highish heels. For ten years after her marriage she was, indeed, the only young duchess in town, the cynosure of as many eyes as her grand-daughter-in-law, Princess Diana, is today. That imposed its responsibilities, and she accepted them and lived up to them. She went to Norman Hartnell for her clothes because she liked him and he was a neighbour of her parents in Bruton Street. He dressed her as she wished to be dressed: not as an ambitious leader of fashion, although he gave her some stunning gowns, but as someone of recognisable identity and taste whom the crowds came to see and were never disappointed, and in styles that her husband and family liked and never disapproved of.

Her state visit to Paris before the war was the biggest challenge of all. It was essential to improve the alliance with France if there were to be a common cause against the Axis powers. But her mother died. The

Below: Queen Elizabeth arriving at Versailles in her famous white dress in July, 1938.
Opposite: The Queen Mother photographed by Anthony Buckley in the drawing-room at Clarence House in May, 1963.

importance of the visit meant it could not be put off. Yet a Queen in dark mourning was not what the critical French were expecting to see. The problem was solved, brilliantly, by her dressing in white, which promptly became an accepted colour for such times. Since she was at her most diplomatic and spoke good French too, it was all a success. Since then she has become, of course, a fashion in herself, which is in many ways the biggest social success of all. If she did not dress as she does, unhappy crowds would go away not quite believing they had seen the Queen Mother they admire. She who, the Girl Guides apart, has never worn uniform, has devised the most distinctive uniform in the land. Her clothes, she has openly and wittily admitted, are her 'props'. Her public would not have it otherwise; and she knows them.

She has always known the value of a good photographer. First, it was Lisa Sheridan who did so well with her daughters; but it was Cecil Beaton who knew precisely what was wanted and delivered it with consummate skill and sense of drama. For the big occasion there has never been anyone, not even Lord Snowdon, in the same league. That was especially important. The image of monarchy in the illustrated papers of the 1930s and 1940s set the tone. She has always been good to press photographers, catching shots for tomorrow's paper. She understands, with unequalled experience, what they want. They feel she will do her best for them. It is a partnership of trust; and it gets results.

She has handled the ups and downs in the life of her second daughter, Princess Margaret, with sympathy and love, although also with a slight bafflement that fate should have been so unkind to someone with so many talents. She looked after her grandchildren in their youth, especially during their parents' absences abroad, with affection and success – which has made the failure of the Princess Royal's marriage and the resultant separation, which is expected to end in divorce, another source of sadness. They have felt, as they have said in their varying ways, that the worst thing they could possibly do would be to let her down.

When George VI died she was reluctant to be called the Queen Mother. Her correct designation is Queen Elizabeth, and that is what her household and Ruffs Guide to the Turf call her. But that was one battle she was never going to be able to win. By common consent she has long become the Queen Mum, an unofficial post that could not have been invented for anyone else, but which she adorns as if she had invented it herself. It is probably a hundred times more important than that of, say, the Lord Warden of the Cinque Ports, which also was awarded her in an inspired bit of casting. Nations are judged by those they take to their hearts. It would be a worry to a number of popular, and not-so-popular, papers if she did not exist. It is not a hype or vulgar adulation, it is meant, and it is one of the better traits of the British that they do mean it.

If she ever does think what her life, and her husband's, would have been like if they had never come to the throne, she shows no sign of regretting what might have been. No doubt she would have done what she does best. She would still have collected Chelsea porcelain with an expert's eye. She would still have trained her eldest grandson to cast a fly and land a salmon. She would still have enjoyed Covent Garden and the music of Benjamin Britten. She would still have bought the paintings of Sydney Nolan. She might even have qualified for the job of governor-general of a Commonwealth country that would have suited

Above: The first three pictures in this sequence recall the wedding of the Queen Mother's grandson, Prince Charles, to Lady Diana Spencer. The others were taken on the day of the christening of her great-grandson, Prince William. The Queen Mother's famous charm failed to silence the squawling infant, but the Princess of Wales soon found a way.

her, had there been the opportunity and had she not been needed here. She has certainly made an excellent and popular university chancellor.

But in the simple things, the things that matter, the things that plain people remember, no one else could have fielded so well and so characteristically the enthusiastic question of a young boy, several years ago, who said to her: 'I've just met your daughter. Do you know she's the Queen?' 'Yes,' she said, 'isn't it exciting!' Without her, there certainly wouldn't have been so much excitement.

Birthdays Past

The following pages show portraits of the Queen Mother taken to commemorate her birthdays.
Below: On her 60th birthday with Prince Charles, Princess Anne and the infant Prince Andrew.
Bottom and right: Two portraits taken by Cecil Beaton at Royal Lodge, Windsor on her 70th birthday.

Two contrasting photographs taken by Norman Parkinson at Clarence House on the Queen Mother's 75th birthday.

Norman Parkinson was again chosen as the official photographer for the Queen Mother's 80th birthday.

The Service of Thanksgiving on July 15, 1980 in honour of the Queen Mother's 80th birthday. The Queen Mother and other members of the Royal Family appeared later on the balcony of Buckingham Palace.

The Queen, Princess Margaret, the Prince and Princess of Wales and Lady Sarah Armstrong-Jones accompany the Queen Mother to the gates of Clarence House to greet the crowd on her 83rd birthday.

CHAPTER SEVEN

'How are my darlings?'

Left: This picture of the Queen Mother at the Derby shows that her interest in horses does not stop at thoroughbred champions.
Below: Days at the races. Top left shows the Queen Mother with Devon Loch, tragic loser of the 1956 Grand National. The remaining pictures show the Queen Mother greeting admirers in the paddock at the National Hunt Festival, Cheltenham; watching a race's progress with fellow turf supporters and in the last picture one of her favourite duties, presenting the cup to the winner.

National Hunt racing is unanimous about one thing: just about the best bit of luck it has had since the war is that the Queen Mother took it up. It was the late Lord Mildmay, himself one of the greatest patrons and bravest riders the sport has had, who put the idea to the then Queen and Princess Elizabeth when he was staying at Windsor for Royal Ascot: would they ever think of owning a jumper? They did. The result was Monaveen, trained for them by Peter Cazalet, and a winner, in Princess Elizabeth's colours, at little Fontwell Park in October, 1949. It was the start of something big.

Racing, of course, was in the blood. The King had an interest in the Flat, although his best horses, Sun Chariot and Big Game, were on the course only for the unofficial, wartime classics at Newmarket; even so, his Hypericum had won the post-war Thousand Guineas in 1946. That was the way the Princess's interest was to turn when she inherited the royal stable from him and sent out a succession of splendid horses like Aureole, Carrozza, Pall Mall, Highclere and the great Dunfermline. But racing was also very much in the Queen Mother's family. The Strathmores had always produced good horsemen, and one of her

kinsmen, John Bowes, had been the first winner of the Triple Crown in 1853 with West Australian; he had, indeed, won the Derby four times, which not even Edward VII was able to do.

Monaveen went on to win the first Queen Elizabeth chase at the old Hurst Park course and was even fancied by some for the Grand National. That did not happen, but his successor, Manicou, was good enough to take the King George VI chase at Kempton on Boxing Day, 1950. That highly popular early success was not followed up in the top division. Racing is like that: for the Queen Mother it was to become

Left: The Riddle of Devon Loch: This sequence of pictures shows Devon Loch running to apparent victory in the 1956 Grand National with Dick Francis aboard. Suddenly he starts to jump over an imaginary fence. The water jump is on the other side of the post at precisely the point where he begins his jump. The next two pictures show Devon Loch in full flight and then spread-eagled on the ground. In the last black and white picture the water jump beyond the post is clearly shown. The modern picture shows the jockey and now famous author, Dick Francis.

only too much like that. The tale of Devon Loch will always be told as long as there is a Grand National. In 1956, clearly in the lead and going easily after two circuits of tremendous, faultless jumping, Devon Loch suddenly faltered and fell on the long run-in, apparently trying to jump a phantom fence. Or so it seemed. Dick Francis, his jockey, has always been inclined to believe that it was the sudden, overwhelming, sound of the whole of the Aintree stands cheering home the royal winner that so startled Devon Loch that he lost his footing. Watching were the Queen, the Queen Mother, Princess Margaret and even Georgi Malenkov, briefly Stalin's successor, who was touring the country. The shouting of the crowd fell away to silence.

The Queen Mother's poise and sportsmanship were never seen better. She went down smiling to congratulate the owner of the winner, ESB, and to console, as only she could, her own people who felt as if their world had come to an end. She said: 'That's racing, I suppose.' Four days later she went to the stables at Fairlawne and saw Devon Loch looking fit and well. She gave Dick Francis a cheque and a silver cigarette box as a memento of the race they had all but won. She is, of course, a devoted reader of the annual novels of racing skulduggery that Francis now writes.

There have been over 350 winners in her colours – the Strathmore ones, naturally, blue, buff stripes, black cap with gold tassel – to make up for that disappointment. But, over the years, it seemed that she would never come as close again to winning a really big race. There were good horses. Tammuz won the Schweppes Gold Trophy at Newbury in 1975. Game Spirit came third in the Cheltenham Gold Cup in 1974. In the Champion Hurdle her Worcran was third in 1965 and David Mould rode her Makaldar into second place in 1967 and Escalus into third in 1970. But luck had turned its face away.

Then, at Sandown Park, one of her favourite courses, on April 28, 1984, it happened. In the Whitbread Gold Cup, the last big steeplechase of the season, her Special Cargo, lame for two years previously, seemed to be doing no more than an honest job when,

Right: On a cold December day the Queen Mother paid one of her many private visits to Sandown Park with her friend and lady-in-waiting, Lady Fermoy.

Above: Studies in concentration of a keen racegoer. The last picture shows the Queen Mother discussing form with Lord Gormley.
Below: The Queen Mother's horse Sun Rising, and jockey, Willie Smith, receive her congratulations after finishing a good second.

with just two fences to go, he and his jockey, Kevin Mooney, found the extra zip that confounds everything in the book. There had to be a photograph and the commentator, Brough Scott, felt in his heart it would be unfair for any horse to lose after such a finish. But the crowd cheered to the skies when Special Cargo got it, and his special owner, in pale blue, descended happily to the winner's enclosure. 'When it comes to prize-givings I'm usually on the other side of the counter,'

The Queen Mother congratulating her horse, Special Cargo who has just won the Whitbread Gold Cup under jockey Kevin Mooney in 1984.

she said. It was the trainer, Fulke Walwyn's, seventh Whitbread; it was her first – and a famous one. What was more, Special Cargo decided to make a habit of winning at Sandown.

It is, actually, not so much on those days that she matters as she does to the sport. Nor is it at Ascot, where she loyally follows her daughter on the Flat after Prince Philip and Prince Charles have made their excuses and left. It is when the sleet is driving across the paddock at Newbury or the rain has turned the little, local track at Windsor into a wallow of mud that the indomitable figure, in rain hat, raincoat and overshoes, leads the umbrellas down from posh boxes to where the horses and the punters are. That is when everyone on the course knows again she is one of theirs.

She is the patron of the Injured Jockeys Fund. She is interested in all her horses and watches over them. Cazalet, her first trainer, said she was apt to ring up to ask: 'How are my darlings?'. At Ascot, at Christmas-time, she has been known to hand out Father Christmas's sweets and presents to the children. The 'blower', the broadcast service that went into every betting shop in the land, was installed in Clarence House, and now televised racing has no more regular a devotee, so that she can keep track of what is happening from Perth south to Folkestone. When she saw the film of the fight against cancer by the National Hunt jockey, Bob Champion, those with her saw tears in her eyes. She is simply devoted to the game, as it is to her.

CHAPTER EIGHT

'That valiant woman'

She likes keeping busy. Whether or not she has been exactly pleased about the idea of international recognition of a ninetieth birthday, she never had any chance of escaping it. These things are determined by the wishes of a loyal public and by television and newspapers that recognise a success, and a popular story, when they see it. So the whole country is joining in, with special celebrations in London, in Scotland, of course, and in Wales. The Lord Mayor of London is giving her lunch at Guildhall. All her 21 regiments and service units, including those from Canada, Australia and New Zealand, will salute her at Horse Guards, including the crews of the aircraft carrier Ark Royal and the submarine Resolution, which she launched. (She has made a particular habit of launching Ark Royals.) A Banqueting House reception and a gala at the Palladium also make it a busy birthday year – even before her birthday.

She is looked for on every great occasion. It was so when she was young. It is so now. Whom did she come with? Who is she talking to? What is she wearing? On state occasions her memories go back further, nowadays, than anyone's. She knew the Australia and New Zealand of the 1920s. She knew the politicians of the 1930s – and even the least successful of them earned her commiseration, and recognition for what they had tried to do. Chamberlain got a kind note of gratitude. De Gaulle was to remember that, whatever else he got in London in the war, he had nothing but courtesy from the King and Queen. After the war, there were meetings with the admiring Smuts, on the last royal tour of South Africa; a conversation with Molotov, the Soviet foreign minister, at a palace evening; and now the evident respect of state visitors from around the world for whom afternoon tea at Clarence House is an essential hour of their time in London.

She has been faithful to her friends, old and new. When they put the stone in the floor of Westminster Abbey in memory of Noel Coward she was there. She has gone back to Northern Ireland, which she first visited with her husband in 1924, to see its people and the men of her regiments even when the plans have leaked out in advance. She went to Oslo for King Olav's eightieth birthday (he is still 36th in line for the

Below left: The Queen Mother, magnificently bejewelled, in Norway with King Olav on the occasion of his birthday.
Below right: The Queen Mother is Patron of the King's Lynn Arts Festival which she attends every July. She is seen here applauding a Mozart concert, performed by the Gabrieli Quartet.
Opposite: The Queen Mother on her annual visit to the Garden of Remembrance at St. Margaret's, Westminster.

Above: The Queen Mother was, for 25 years, the Chancellor of London University. On the day she stepped down from that position she was presented with this portrait by Michael Noakes.
Left: The Queen Mother and the Prince and Princess of Wales are greeted by Lord Delfont at a Royal Variety Performance.

Below: The Queen Mother always enjoys her journeys by helicopter. She is seen here arriving at the Isle of Sark in May, 1984.

British throne). She was there on Britannia when the QE2 returned to Southampton from the Falklands. The Smithfield show simply would not know what to do without her. When the Crazy Gang, whom she and her husband enjoyed so much, was down to one survivor, Chesney Allen, she was there for the gala performance of 'Underneath the Arches'. There was almost consternation when it was thought she might not be able to go to the wedding of the Prince and Princess of Wales. She missed the fireworks in Hyde Park but she was happily at St Paul's, Prince Edward at her side, in the carriage.

This is precisely what she has always gladly promised the country. In what are now the thirty-eight years of her widowhood she has managed to fulfil even the expectations that surround her every appearance. It may have come out that she does not particularly

Above: On April 25, 1988 the Queen Mother spent a full day with the Light Infantry, of which she is Colonel-in-Chief, at the Sir John Moore Barracks in Hampshire.

Below: Each year on St Patrick's Day the Queen Mother exchanges shamrock sprays with the Irish Guards.

admire Mr. Tony Benn or General Idi Amin or former President Carter (whose too-cousinly kiss she did not appreciate), but they seem to be about all that she does not like. It is perfectly possible that she is not alone in her views of them – or in her evident enjoyment of Jaguar cars (the XJ12 has been particularly admired for its speed), and helicopters and dancing. These are creditable tastes for a nonagenarian. She does now think there is too much television of indifferent quality, but television is forgiven much when it replays entertaining old films: 'Whisky Galore' and other Ealing comedies are always welcome.

The Queen Mother in Toronto in July 1989 with the Governor-General, Madam Sauvé. This trip celebrated the 50th anniversary of her first visit to Canada.

No year finds her idle, or out of the news. There are her good causes and her regiments to look after. There are her continuing visits abroad, including yet another one to Canada last summer, on the fiftieth anniversary of her first visit with the King in 1939. The Canadians did her proud, bringing out again the vintage open limousine in which she was driven then. When one of the ceremonies went on and on, the heat seemed oppressive and the media said she looked tired and bothered for a moment. She told everyone not to fuss. And, of course, there were the races at Woodbine, in Toronto, and a new Canadian triple crown winner, With Approval, to cheer her up.

She went back to the East End after many years, to talk about memories of the war with Charlie Lunn of Lunn's Caff; he promised her a proper breakfast for £1.50. She went to see The Times again, and the Red Arrows. She unveiled the memorial to Lord Dowding, the commander-in-chief, Fighter Command, during the Battle of Britain. After the war the King had been worried that Dowding had never been properly honoured for his part in the victory, so her gesture was meant to help to right a wrong that had troubled him. And "a little older and perhaps a little wiser" as she put it, she spoke to the last Land Army reunion in Birmingham.

There were her hospital wards to fight for. There was even a portrait by a young artist, Alison Watt, which was meant, Ms Watt said, to demystify both the monarchy and her. The sitter's fans were angry about it: she did not seem to mind at all. There were gardens to visit and enjoy, and family occasions, and children, and the regular dates which would just not have been the same without her.

Every birthday now has been turned, in its way, into a special, happy, informal royal ceremony. The eightieth one was nearly as special as this year's, with a service at St Paul's, a rose walk planted in St James's Park just across the way from her, a garden party at the palace, an evening at Covent Garden. But each birthday morning there is the mail, arriving in sackfuls, the band playing 'Happy Birthday' outside, the children with flowers and an eagerness to catch her eye, and her daughters and a scattering of grandchildren there to do her honour.

Over all the years that she has been in the public eye, whether she liked it or not, she has devoted to her job all that her temperament, her upbringing, her charm, her sense of duty, her unrivalled experience, and her flair have given her. It was her favourite photographer, Cecil Beaton, who spotted part of it. 'There is,' he said 'something of the great actress about her.' It could not have been otherwise. There is little point, as Bagehot said, in having a court if it is a dull court. All the time she has found the confidence to be herself, to do and say what has been distinctive to her.

Below: The Queen Mother surrounded by well-wishers on her 84th birthday.

Above: The Queen Mother is Patron of the London Gardens Society and each summer she visits London gardens, both large and small.

It has not always worked. When she was first engaged, she felt entirely capable of dealing with the newspapers. She saw the man from the *Star* by herself, at home. He promptly asked how often the Duke of York had proposed to her. She replied crisply: 'Now look at me. Do you think I am the sort of person Bertie would have to ask twice?' It was good stuff, but it appalled George V, unaccustomed to any badinage like that, who declared there would be no more interviews. That was a pity. More of her candour would have enlightened and cheered up the nation. But she has been chary of interviews ever since.

What has come through has been her instinctive ability to do and say precisely what was needed, and only she has been likely to think of it. On her wedding day at the Abbey in 1923, before she walked up the lengthy aisle, she placed her wedding bouquet on the grave of the Unknown Warrier in front of her. On her first Commonwealth tour, when the battle cruiser Renown had a fire in her boiler room and there was a real danger that it might spread to the oil tanks, she was asked by the captain afterwards if she had known how dangerous it was. 'Yes,' she said, 'every hour someone said there was nothing to worry about, so I knew there was real trouble.' In the war there was her unqualified resolve: 'I shall not go down like the others.' When Devon Loch stumbled within sight of the winning post at Aintree, her first thought was for her jockey and her stable: 'I must go down and comfort those poor people.' And at Frogmore, in 1972, beside the Duke of Windsor's grave, when his widow was distraught, it was the Queen Mother who, after long years, took the Duchess's arm gently and said: 'I know how you feel. I've been through it myself.'

In return, her family and friends have spoken of her with a devotion and a simple eloquence that say all that needs to be said after 85 years.

Her son-in-law, the Earl of Snowdon, after the end of his marriage: 'I have more admiration for her than for anyone else in the world.'

Her grandson, Prince Charles: 'Ever since I can remember, my grandmother has been the most wonderful example of fun, laughter, warmth, infinite security and, above all else, exquisite taste in so many things.'

And Winston Churchill, on the death of her husband: 'That valiant woman who sustained King George through all his toils and problems.'

She is herself. There has been no other.

CHAPTER NINE

Her Contribution to History

What will historians of the future say about her? What will some Walter Bagehot, speculating on the functions and the survival, or otherwise, of the peculiar institutions of the British people, decide about her and her contribution to the monarchy in the twentieth century? He, or she, will probably be clear enough about the contribution to the dignified side of things, but what has it meant in the efficient life of the nation? How much of it has she done by chance, by personality, or by design, by calculation? She does not particularly enjoy delving back into the past herself.

Her life has coincided with this century's for all but seven months, far longer already than Queen Victoria's ever coincided with the nineteenth. But her name, unlike Victoria's, is not joined, nor will it be joined, with the name of the century or any particularly great cause or movement or transformation in it. Centuries are busier now; royal figures are less influential. It hasn't really been in her nature, or in her job, to dominate. All her days her job has been strictly limited: to inhibit radical change, the change that would damage the monarchy. Nothing much else is expected from monarchs and even less from Queen Mothers. The one British monarch of the century who talked much of change, and even played at it, was Edward VIII.

Left: In July, 1985 the Queen Mother visited small gardens in south London.
Below: At the Trooping the Colour ceremony on June 17, 1989 the Queen Mother shared a carriage with the Princess of Wales and Princes William and Henry.

Right: The Duchess of York with her daughters and the Duchess of Kent in St Paul's Cathedral during celebrations for King George V's Silver Jubilee in May 1935. The Duke of York and Duke of Kent are seen in the background.

Adaptability has been her strength in warding off damaging change: careful, considered, even stylish. She has given her job meaning and warmth, her own meaning, her own warmth. The very words Queen Mother now have a connotation that is indistinguishable from her own personality. For generations the British called the widows of kings Queen Dowager. Of the two preceding Queen Mothers no one expected very much and certainly not modernisation of any kind.

No one in the chattering classes expected much from Queen Elizabeth either. They had thought her and her own family, the Strathmores, unremarkable. She had been remorselessly patronised as Duchess of York, held to be charming but unimportant. The reality of monarchy and its future had been with her brother-in-law. It was only when that ended, suddenly and irretrievably, that she got her proper job, real, urgent and unwelcome as it was.

It was in her nature to succeed at it, and her success has scotched one myth about the royal family and the royal way of life: that only those who had had a lifetime's training for the job could do it. Her brother-in-law, the former King who had had a lifetime's training, got it all wrong within a year. Her husband, only half-trained to it, was highly apprehensive about the very idea of taking over. She took to her job by being herself, as in the end her husband did his by being

Left: The Duchess of York photographed by Dorothy Wilding in 1936.

himself. In a real sense they succeeded because of their limitations. It was her common sense not to try to be what they were not. They were not particularly regal or intellectual. But neither were they simply the nice couple with two promising young daughters living in a sort of grandiose south-east semi-detached, as many suburbanites at the time somehow imagined they were. What mattered was that they had successfully adapted to the expectations and imaginations of the suburbs, or, at least, to the expectations of the magazine articles and picture captions which instructed the suburbs on what to expect.

What mattered more was that they were modest enough, for themselves and in their expectations of what they could do, to have an appeal for the people now of most political substance, the working class. Queen Victoria and Edward VII had not worried too much about the masses. George V had been astonished to find that people liked him. The Duke and Duchess of York had actually gone round factories, a real novelty, before they came to the throne. They could look like plain people. The popular papers and the newsreels played it up. Now the monarchy was conscious of the working class, and the friends it had there, in Britain and the Empire, as never before. The masses had entered the royal calculation, and the publicists' calculations, finally and decisively.

This was very much within her compass. She saw plainly that the country of the 1930s was basically disposed to want what her husband wanted: reassurance. It did not want a grand monarchy (and, least of all, a raffish American one); it did not want a bicycling one either. Neither did she, either then or now. It was a country still wounded in

Facing page: King George VI and Queen Elizabeth in a motorcade through Quebec during their visit to Canada in May, 1939.
Below: The King and Queen with the four Canadian Mounted Police who were their bodyguard during their tour.

ntenac GARAGE
WITH A SMILE
ALL NIGHT PARKING AND REPAIRS
PRESTONE

spirit by the losses of the Great War and determined to avoid another if it could. It lived with chronic industrial unrest (Princess Elizabeth had been born on the eve of the General Strike), and outside southern England had still not recovered from the slump. But it still believed it had reason to think of itself as a great power, and it expected its first family to reflect that.

So the new, already adapted (and still adaptable) monarchy was given its chance. Over half a century on, when the greatest public worries about the monarchy are over marriage problems or child care or blood sports, how vulnerable it seems the Crown was thought, and thought itself, to be then. It was not, of course, but one of the reasons was that while the new King was thought to be very like his unimaginative father (a reassurance to some of his subjects), the new Queen was very different indeed from previous ones. Her assets then, as now, were formidable: she was British, she was a commoner, and she was highly sociable, a complete rarity in a family isolated from ordinary life and friendships. It did not hurt that she was not American either.

The very status of a queen had actually changed crucially. To be a consort was now, with her, to be seen to be a self-reliant person. For generations royal consorts, male or female, good or bad, happy or unhappy, had been the creatures of arranged marriages. Queen Mary, her immediate predecessor, had been shifted by Queen Victoria from an arranged marriage to one grandson to an arranged marriage to another. Suddenly it was possible for a king and queen to have

Below: The Queen with her daughters in the grounds of Royal Lodge, Windsor in April, 1940 when Princess Elizabeth was nearly fourteen and Princess Margaret was ten.

Right: Princess Elizabeth attended a course at the Mechanical Transport Training Centre as part of her ATS duties during the war. She is shown here explaining the finer points of the internal combustion engine to her mother.

married for love – provided, of course, they played to the popular rules. This was very much a novelty: an essential footnote to the monarchy's new, populist tract. It also helped that she was known to be a reluctant conscript. However much she liked to be the centre of attention as a child and young woman, there was, and is, no doubt that she had no wish to be Queen. In that sense the country was as lucky to get her as her husband had been told by his father he was.

With these strengths she could set about rebuilding, or at least redecorating, the monarchy. Her convictions about the monarchy and its value are strong, so strong she has never needed to justify them. Whether she has ever worried much about constitutional matters is an open question; whether she has ever felt the lack of the political grounding that only years of experience of state papers gives, or is supposed to give, has probably never worried her. Her husband, who came to the royal homework late, and her daughter who has had to live with it almost all her adult life, both graduated in the affairs of the world with exceptional marks for conscientiousness – something else that Edward VIII entirely lacked, and, in the end, was punished for.

What the Queen Elizabeth of 1936–9 plainly saw was that the perception of the monarchy must be updated without admitting it, that it must depend on the habit of loyalty without calling on it, and that it must project itself by personal example without ever drawing attention to it. Changes that work, and work because they are popular, are usually unformulated. Someone sets out to do what they think has to be done. When it is seen to work they are given the credit, and the whole approach, the whole system alters and adapts to accommodate it. That was precisely what happened in the three years the monarchy had to put itself on a new track before the war came and enveloped everything.

BRIT
RED CROS

Above: The King and Queen with Princess Elizabeth inspecting the Royal Artillery in a scout car.

Because the monarchy relaunched itself by popular permission in these three years, the Queen's part is invariably qualified as shrewd, calculating and remorseless. It probably wasn't as deliberate as that. It probably was just self-defence. But the Duke of Windsor and his wife were the ones who, falling from grace, found themselves implacably out-manoeuvred, ostracised and excluded from the warmth of popular affection and suspended judgment without which no modern royal existence can be tolerable. That it took the Windsors entirely by surprise showed how vulnerable, how paltry a target they really were. Both had counted on his past acceptability, if not his whole popularity, continuing whenever he chose to summon it back. They might have got a long way with George VI on his own, and even with Queen Mary on her own: they could not because someone sufficiently resolute and realistic was holding the anti-Windsor barrier together.

By ensuring that abdicating kings never return Queen Elizabeth set in place another of her own footnotes to the constitution. The Duke of Windsor could not be acceptable as other than an inconsiderable, almost alien figure; his wife could never have a royal title; the power of royal anathema in a democratic age would be demonstrated and entrenched. It was not vindictive, it was essential. She did it and held to it for long enough that in the end there was nothing left between the three except the ultimate exhaustion of forgiveness. But long before then they had won nothing and she had won everything she had needed.

Left: Setting a good example, the Queen is seen carrying a gas mask in a haversack during the first few days of the war in September, 1939.

It showed how she does not forget. But in the first years the best vindication of the new monarchy was not that it kept out Mrs Simpson but that it did positive things, things that the country could understand and respect. When almost every instinct of the intelligentsia was to do

Above: The King and Queen inspecting the damage caused by Luftwaffe bombs to Buckingham Palace in September, 1940.

the obvious things that intelligentsias are keen on, such as speaking up about economics, unemployment, the arms race, the Abyssinians and the Spanish Republicans, precisely the things that monarchies cannot influence and should be deflected from, the King and Queen did the sensible things and did them well.

There was the state visit to Paris: it went off well enough and the Foreign Office congratulated itself and for a moment people were a little more optimistic about avoiding war with Hitler. Little optimism is put into state visits to and from France nowadays; most people in both countries now would never have heard of Edward VII's visit in 1903, greatly admired at the time but which merely gave an elegant, after-dinner endorsement to one new factor in the balance of power. The royal visit in July 1938 helped to hold an irresolute alliance together for some more months; whether it did anything to keep a single French soldier fighting in 1940 is entirely improbable. No one can win them all.

Their next big diplomatic mission abroad was a real success, for two reasons. It did something novel: no reigning King and Queen had been to the United States, or even Canada, before. And the relationship with North America was too important, when the war did begin, for each political community, on both sides of the Atlantic, to dare to allow the visit to fail. In most political worlds there is always something extra for being first. This was not exactly understood by George VI: one of his particular regrets at the outbreak of war was that he would not be able to go to India to repeat his father's ostentatious

Above: The Queen visiting a Convalescent Home for Free French Naval Forces with General de Gaulle and Admiral Musilier in 1941.

success at the Delhi Durbar in 1911. The one, and as it turned out the only, royal British Durbar, had been George V's one great creation ('entirely my own idea') in the brisk manufacture of royal occasions in the first quarter of the century. But in the India of the 1930s it could have led nowhere. The North American visit, overtly political as it was, actually pointed the right way. Whatever the royal family may have thought, or feared, about a formal visit to the United States, it now seems wilfully neglectful that in 1939 nothing of the kind had been done for Canada or Australia or New Zealand. It had been obliging of George V to send his sons and daughters-in-law around the Empire, but the new approach was as overdue as it was essential.

As it turned out, the new monarchy got it right: right in coping with the crowds and the newspaper press, and right in coping with the formidable Roosevelts without affectation or pretension. No great corner in history was actually turned by the royal visit to the Roosevelts, no great decision or friendship was settled. But it certainly helped. A President who had abiding doubts about the British Empire, a King who knew little or nothing of America, were both persuaded that an alliance must be formed and must be upheld because of what the future was bound to bring. It mattered. It had gone off well, and lastingly, because of the King's conviction that the policy was right. The imminent war doubled the influence of the occasion and what it was meant to mean.

An important, perhaps a controlling, influence on the Queen Mother's opinions and memories was decided then. It may be a reflection of her instincts that she has gone back to Canada five times as often as she has to the United States – or to Australia or New Zealand. Canada won her heart then, even, or perhaps because of, the French Canadian complication. It can even help not to be English. Part of it is certainly because of the Scottish connection and her Canadian regiments in the war. What probably matters most is her essential conservatism: the Empire, and then the Commonwealth, has come first, before wider, even more beguiling horizons.

This has not been, and is not, because of doubts or hesitations about the United States. She has enjoyed her visits, imbued as they have been with particular memories, and the Americans have pointed unfailingly to every democratic clue or inkling they find in her (as they respond now to the present Duchess of York). But Canada was more her scene, more her cup of tea. And, besides, her whole experience has been to oppose the Americanisation of the Crown, to be a brake on the occasional enthusiasms of a younger generation drawn that way.

Queen Mothers do not have a great influence on diplomacy, even royal diplomacy. If they had, her influence on, and interest in Rhodesia, and the Central African multi-racial idea would have been interesting and perhaps even important. She plainly believed in it – but it was an activity that was to be found, in the end, to be inconsequential. She has said nothing about that beyond natural regret. She plainly enjoyed her one visit to South Africa before anyone in Britain had ever heard of apartheid. She has been assumed to be a sympathiser with sensible white aspirations; she has also been

Below: Footmen in Dick Turpin cuffs and Tricorns man the carriage in which the Queen Mother toured the colonial town of Williamsburg in Virginia during her visit to the United States in 1954. Beside her is Mr Kenneth Chorley and sitting opposite are her Lady-in-Waiting Mrs John Mulholland and Mr Winthrop Rockefeller.

The Queen Mother, accompanied by the Mayor, waves to schoolchildren during her visit to Queenstown, New Zealand in 1966.

invariably too quick and shrewd with her conversation to be caught unawares or unsuspecting. She has since kept to the straight and narrow of official policy about Africa without evident reservations.

The real diplomatic test was the war. The true diplomacy of constitutional monarchy is with its own people. The treaty between them is complicated: it has innumerable hypothetical, unwritten clauses defining what the people want in return for their allegiance or, if not that, their tolerant respect. A hypothetical clause may be no more than a nuance, but each is an interpretation of what people want in attitudes, behaviour, conformities, definitions, all that a monarchy can voice or represent of past, present and future. It was what the royal family of 1939–45 did well, and is held to have done well, in everyone's most difficult time, and it is the source to this day of much of more than one generation's respect for the monarchy.

The Queen Mother still embodies much of what the British people and their media still portray as the essential truth of how they won the war. Nowhere is the Queen Mother more invincibly popular than at occasions recalling those days: in the armed services, in the East End of London, on Remembrance Sunday, with the Women's Land Army, with the Australians and Canadians, with the Free French. In a way, nothing should have been simpler then: the royal family as the exemplars of a united and ultimately victorious war effort. But it was not exactly like that then.

In 1940, when the war was going very badly, the Crown was as much in jeopardy as any part of the state. It was, in fact, the symbol of a state that was doing very badly, that could not pretend to defend its people

Above: In 1988 the Queen Mother watched the Remembrance Day service from a Foreign Office balcony in Whitehall accompanied by the Princess of Wales, Prince Edward, the Duchess of York and the Princess Royal.

from, it seemed, unremitting air attack. The Blitz, the firebomb raids, on London and provincial cities, did not actually see all the British at their best. The fabric of their lives was collapsing, as was their civil defence; people refused to come out of deep shelters, people refused to go back to their cities and homes, observers reported nothing short of a lack of will to go on.

This was what underlay the exchanges that entered the anecdote of those days: the Queen who felt able to look the East End in the face was only too conscious she had been jeered there, that it had been the idle joke about the East End that the Germans ought to have had the sense not to bomb west of London Bridge and there would have been a revolution. Fewer than 20 years before, in the face of the first Bolsheviks, the Crown had been preoccupied, and as far as its continental cousins were concerned, inhibited, immobilised, even unable to save those cousins who had fought on the Allied side, by just such fears.

The daily royal journey from Windsor to a smouldering London, the succession of obligatory visits to cities that lacked the will to go on, was an unending test of diplomatic skills with the British, it was an unending test of royal willpower. It was the front on which the war could be lost. It was where the monarchy, any monarchy, had a part, a duty, to play.

In the revolutions of 1848 the Queen of Prussia told Bismarck that her husband had been sleepless in the crisis. He had replied conclusively: 'Madam, kings should be able to sleep.' It was in ensuring that, besides plain people's sleep, that Queen Elizabeth earned her war memoirs. In that sense, in the bombed ruins she stood among to comfort and console and be photographed (all three were equal in the war effort), it was the first time a queen had gone to war in Britain since the first Elizabeth went down to Tilbury to make a speech hardly anyone heard. But then the first Elizabeth did not have too many media to satisfy. It was the first time a king and queen had stood on a battlefield together; the last king had been George II at Dettingen in 1743, but he had been defending Hanover.

Right: Queen Elizabeth in a 1948 study by Cecil Beaton.

Royal Style

The Queen Mother's sense of style in her clothes has remained distinctive over the years. The general themes and colours have changed little despite the fashions of the day. Her first great fashion 'success' was during her visit to Paris with King George VI in 1938 when she dazzled the French in a series of Norman Hartnell creations.

These four pages contain a selection of photographs taken over a period of 55 years. They show a unique flair for 'public' fashion which has been the Queen Mother's hallmark. The finishing touches to her outfits are a string of beautiful pearls and a carefully chosen diamond brooch.

The Queen Mother has become particularly noted over the years for her hats, each designed to accompany a specific outfit and the colour carefully chosen. In 1969, at the suggestion of Norman Hartnell, she began her association with the milliner Rudolf whose hats she wore until his death in 1980. Since then her hats have been designed by Rudolf's partner, Joy Quested-Nowell.

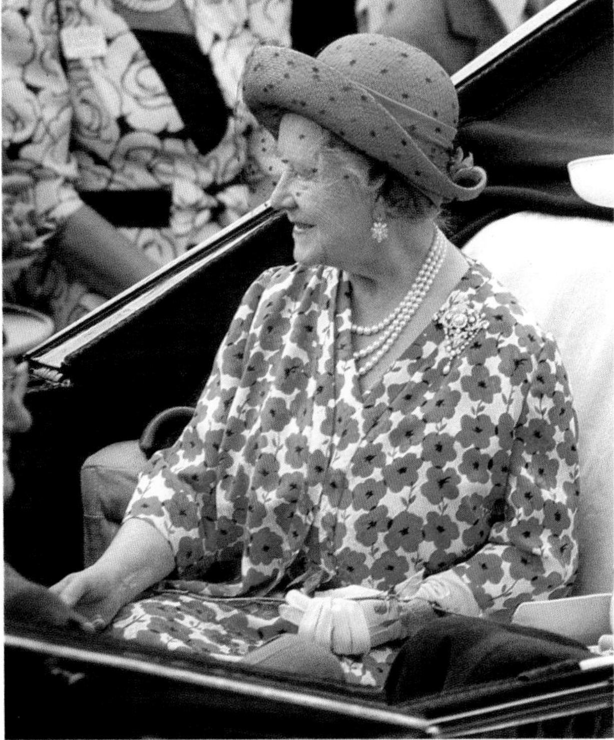

CHAPTER TEN

The Unending Test

The media have always liked the Queen Mother, and she has been scrupulously careful never, or hardly ever, to show any doubts about them. She has always had the style that takes the media attention for granted. The attention is part of the job, and the only real way to do the job is to meld and merge with the attention, as she does, to carry everything off as a great, new, unsurpassed production. Her shrewdness shows through. She has, of course, very shrewd advisers and helpers, loyally directed by Sir Martin Gilliat, her private secretary since 1956, who chooses to stay out of the limelight: their unobtrusiveness is the longest-playing act in the game. They have decided and agree, over the years, on the essentials that bring success – and have claimed no credit for it.

The first requirement is considered availability: not too frequent, not too infrequent, not always doing the favourite or obvious things but never neglecting the things expected of her. Stills photography and film, especially silent film, suited her well, and still do. Radio she was cautious about, even when it was required of her in the war: radio asks everything of a voice. Television has its appeal for her, but with limits. It is the words that are managed best: there are selectively few

Below: The Queen Mother has been a patron of the Royal Caledonian Schools in Bushey, Hertfordshire since 1937. The school is for the children of the officers and men of Scottish regiments. This photograph was taken at the dedication of the 'Hall of Regiments' in 1989.
Right: The Queen Mother attended the official opening of a new wing of Queen Charlotte's Hospital in May, 1989.

Above and left: The Queen Mother, radiant as ever, on the occasion of her 89th birthday at Clarence House.

of them, as there have been all along. She is not strong on original words and ideas and has never attempted them: they are left to the Prince of Wales and other people's speech writers. She gives her audiences what they expect: reminiscence, proper sentiment, a little self-effacement, a sense of occasion and wellbeing. But it is never too long, just as the exchanges used in the television clips are not too long. She has adapted, as if by instinct, to the requirements of the principal medium. She does not give even brief interviews. Her words are private, not public.

Her clothes are public, hardly private. They are still, as they have always been, her distinctive touch. With them there can be no imitations, and the themes and colours have stayed unchanged over the years. That is the mark of star quality: to persist with caricature. Hers is, of course, acceptable and affectionate; caricature is what royal

Left: The Queen Mother receiving flowers from children on her 89th birthday.

families can probably do without, but dealing with it is part of the basic royal diplomacy of the times. The royal family has had, and has, its members who do not keep up with the times, do not understand them, do not want to understand them; and when they do they fail to notice where the media have misled them.

The signs have long been accumulating that the Queen Mother's way is probably not the winning way for the modern family, or is certainly not likely to be for much longer. Institutions have to change at the right pace to survive. Parliaments have to learn to live with television, popes have to have the gift of languages, empires have to come to terms with nationalities. The Queen Mother's style, her ways, have served her and her times. She epitomises the development of the monarchy's set piece range, the importance attached to royal weddings, occasions, anniversaries. Her poise, her gestures, her very facial expressions are part and parcel of a theatre now at the height of its art. But it may not be an art that is changing appreciably enough for the 1990s. Commonwealth formalities, such as the heads of government meetings, are left severely to the Queen's own judgment: it is, after all, a personal commitment of hers. Britain in Europe has had no royal ceremonial recognition, or has not been allowed any. That way forward seems limited.

To the Queen Mother, indeed, have been left many of what seem safely dull occasions, including pointless theatrical ones that must often make her yearn for another quiet evening at home. No one could do the informality routines with more charm or tact. But her young people are now normally very young indeed, as at her birthday appearances at the gates of Clarence House. There may be an understandable reluctance to expose her to the more unbearable of

Below: The Queen Mother is joined by the Queen, the Prince and Princess of Wales, the Duke and Duchess of York, Prince Edward, Viscount Linley and Lady Sarah Armstrong-Jones as she acknowledges the crowd of well-wishers on her 89th birthday.

Right: Princess Margaret and the Earl of Snowdon visiting the Queen Mother at Clarence House with the infant Viscount Linley in 1961.

student efforts at self-expression, but the sure-footed, disarmingly-spoken Chancellor of London University from 1955 to 1980 may have been under-used since. When there had been bad troubles in Brixton she was much the best choice to soothe the ruffled and reassure the anxious, but, again, the anxious were chiefly among the original West Indian immigrants more disposed to social stability than their children. Such is the diplomacy of appearance and gesture.

Now, in the last decade of the century, the movers and pushers who like to think they advise the monarchy are intent on modernising it again their way, to suit the habits and morals of another generation that is impressed by opinion polls and headline speculation. The Queen is told it would be popular if she were to abdicate; Princess Anne is often said, with press approval, to be wanting a divorce from her husband, just as her aunt Margaret was divorced from hers. So divorce and abdication, the two issues that actually brought George VI and the Queen Mother to the throne in 1936 are plainly given a very different royal connotation today.

This is going to be a problem. Divorce is not, actually, on the increase, and three-quarters of the country still professes itself wanting to see more safeguards for marriage. But the prospects of more royal marriages ending in divorce and, no doubt, in remarriage have multiplied exponentially since the 1930s. To people of the Queen Mother's generation this was unthinkable even as late as Princess Margaret's decision not to marry Group Captain Peter Townsend in 1955. That has evidently gone by the board now, but with no guidelines on what may be right, morally, materially or even, one day, constitutionally. It may be possible to accept that Princess Margaret

Above: For her birthday treat in 1987 the Queen Mother was given a flight in Concorde accompanied by Viscount Linley, Lady Sarah Armstrong-Jones and Susannah Constantine.

and the Princess Royal are now so far from the succession that it does not matter. But what if modern opinion were widely opposed to priority being given to males against females? Whatever the complications of 1936, those were essentially simple days.

History is always being rewritten. It is a nice question if a modern generation will ever come to think that Edward VIII should have kept his throne if such ideas become commonly accepted. And if that were to be, so history might take a different view of what the Queen Mother's principles and work have been worth. It would be a verdict of hindsight only, but there have been stranger ones in a perverse world. It is still some way off. The same opinion polls that approve or accept royal abdication and divorce still put the Queen Mother herself first in public popularity.

Still, things are changing from her way, her outlook. Year by year as the century has progressed the perceived importance of the central figures of the monarchy has declined, and the perceived importance of the elected politicians has grown. The politicians, naturally enough, have seen nothing wrong whatever in this. They show courtesy and deference to the royal family, or at least to those members of it that are held to matter. They are partial to royal occasions that increase the dignity and popularity of the state, and thus of themselves, its political representatives. Royalty is even welcome from time to time on the White House lawn. But it is difficult to think of a politician this century, even Churchill during the war, who has not acted as if the monarch were secondary, a walk-on player, there to do his or her constitutional job, and certainly not there to cause trouble or waste ministerial time.

The television spectacles politicians prefer are summit meetings,

The Queen Mother chatted with pop star Kylie Minogue at the Royal Variety Performance in 1988.

addresses to the United Nations, and European Community, Nato and all other kinds of conferences. It began with Versailles in 1919, with the League of Nations: so it had begun to eclipse royalty in the Queen Mother's youth and it has increased decade by decade. And it is more important than just an interesting family on the throne, if usually not so much fun. There are ways, of course, for a monarchy to recapture attention and interest besides spectacle and media gossip. If royal voices cannot talk about party political issues, then intelligent and fashionable concern about world environment, world health, world hunger and world poverty are still permissible – the way the Prince of Wales and the Princess Royal have taken.

That way accedes to the liberal moods and sweeping generalities of the times. The Queen Mother's way has been very different. The impact she made on the debate on the health service was influential simply because she kept her eye on the issue to specifics: one in 1988 was the closure of a hospital ward for the elderly at Merthyr Tydfil which she had opened less than a year before. She let it be known to the authorities that she was 'saddened, distressed and upset' at the news. She got a letter of explanation from the Secretary of State for Wales, and the ward was saved. No one said it was politics, but it was very practical politics. So was her letter to York council on the closing of Brackenhill home for old people. A stiff word, or even a diplomatic word, for one of her interests can bring results.

What she has done over the years is precisely what Bagehot advised over a century ago when he said royalty had the right to be consulted, the right to encourage, and the right to warn. That has become an article of faith. But Bagehot went on to say what was, and is, more important: that in confronting a minister with an effective argument, a

Right: The Queen and Queen Mother compare racing notes at the Derby in 1988.

king might not always turn the politician's course, 'but he would always trouble his mind'. Troubling a politician's mind, drawing on an unrivalled memory and experience, is the real weapon of the modern Crown. Putting doubts into people's minds, even when not flatly opposing them, is something at which the Queen Mother is adept.

The deepest fear of a royal family is that democratic politicians will one day find it politic to set up a royal commission into the royal family. Even if the commission gets nowhere, even if its report is ignored or outvoted, some of the allegory, some of the myth, some of the sensible and useful work of the monarchy, some of its very meaning, will have been lost. It is likely to happen over money one day; another abdication could prompt it; an abdication like that of 1936 certainly would prompt it. It has been her lifelong contribution in keeping that family mortification away that the Queen Mother has achieved her purpose. She knows that the family can survive disappointment in individuals, even the failure of individual careers and marriages, if the integral family stays unharmed. In the nature of life there will be failures: no family can produce repeated success as kings, dukes or princesses. The Queen Mother, who has been there to pick up the pieces in the past, and remembers that, has known that better than anyone.

A queen consort has to bring many qualities to her marriage and to her realm. It is important that her style, her appearance, is to the country's liking. If she cannot gain the country's ear, then she can still regularly catch its eye. If her husband is cleverer than she, then she has fulfilled her duty by her face and form, her sympathy and her children. If she is cleverer than her husband (and it has frequently been so) then she is wise to ensure that her marriage is seen to be one of equals, and nothing more. But it normally shows.

Right: The Queen Mother welcomes the Queen to Scrabster in northern Scotland in August, 1986. The Queen, who had been cruising to the Western Isles in HMS Britannia, *travelled to the Castle of Mey, her mother's Scottish home, where they were joined by other members of the royal family for lunch.*

The Queen Mother accompanied by Prince Charles as they walk in procession to St George's Chapel for the Garter ceremony in June, 1987.

The British monarchy has been run by dominant females for a century and a half: Victoria, Queen Mary (much cleverer than her husband), the Queen Mother and the present Queen. It remains to be seen if women – the great majority of those who take an active interest in the monarchy – will ever get tired of a matriarchy. What matters, and what is most appreciated in the unending diplomacy between royalty and public is the perception and practice of loyalty, even the loyalty of long-forgotten queens, Carolines, Charlottes, Adelaides, that modern women would say was for kings entirely undeserving of it.

Queen Elizabeth's essential contribution to the monarchy of the twentieth century has been made irrefutable by the monarchy's continuance and acceptance by popular will. She has given her family the chance to stay in touch with opinions and ideals, to adapt, communicate, work and plan into the twenty-first century; and that means, for her and her daughter, the continuing opportunity to succeed in the endless test of the Crown's purpose and endurance.

Overleaf: Bedecked by flowers and flags, the Queen Mother bids farewell to the crowds who had gathered to wish her a happy 89th birthday.